A Student Guide to
SPSS

— Carrie Cuttler

University of British Columbia

Kendall Hunt
publishing company
4050 Westmark Drive • P O Box 1840 • Dubuque IA 52004-1840

Cover Image © Shutterstock, Inc.

Kendall Hunt
publishing company

www.kendallhunt.com
Send all inquiries to:
4050 Westmark Drive
Dubuque, IA 52004-1840

Contents

4   Regression   41

5   Sign Test   51

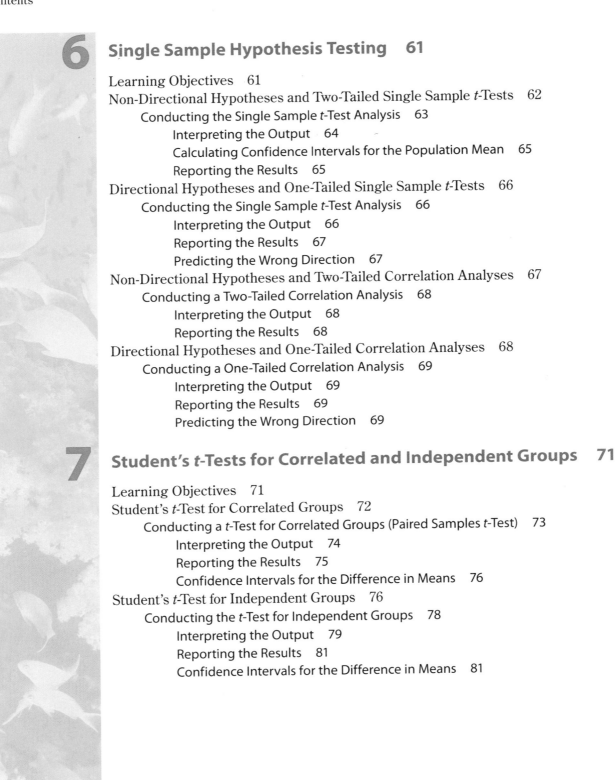

reface

SPSS stands for Statistical Package for the Social Sciences. As its name implies, the software was developed for use in the social sciences, and it is currently one of the most commonly used statistical software packages in psychology, business, education, and market research. The popularity of SPSS is likely a result of its intuitive drop down menus that allow for quick and easy computation of the most commonly used statistics. This guide will provide you with easy-to-follow, step-by-step instructions on how to execute some of the most commonly used functions in SPSS, as well as how to interpret the results. While it was originally developed for use in introductory statistics courses, it should be beneficial to anyone who needs to become familiar with the program.

This guide is packaged with a copy of PASW Statistics Student Version 18. Do not be concerned about this difference in name. IBM acquired SPSS in October 2009. Shortly after its acquisition, IBM gave the software a minor facelift and changed its name to PASW Statistics (PASW stands for Predictive Analytics Software). Since then IBM has decided to revert back to the original name, and future versions of the software will be named SPSS. As such, I will stick with tradition and will refer to the program as SPSS throughout this guide. Differences between the various versions of SPSS (and PASW) tend to be slight, so this guide should be of practical use for any version of SPSS or PASW you need to learn to use.

An Introduction to SPSS

Learning Objectives

In this chapter you will learn how to install and open SPSS. You will learn how to create variables, define the properties of those variables, and enter data into SPSS. You will also learn some handy tools and tricks for manipulating and transforming data.

Getting Started

Installing SPSS

The disk packaged with this guide is compatible for use with Microsoft® Windows® 7, Windows XP and Windows Vista® or Apple® Mac 10.5x (Leopard™) and 10.6x (Snow Leopard™). The software expires 13 months after installation, it can only be installed twice, and it is limited to 50 variables (columns) and 1500 cases (rows). Before attempting to install SPSS you must first be logged onto your computer with administrator privileges. To install the software simply insert the disk and follow the onscreen instructions.

Opening SPSS

To open SPSS go to **Start → Programs → SPSS Inc → PASW Statistics 18 → PASW Statistics Student Version**. A window like the one shown below should now appear. It provides you with several options, including options to run a tutorial, type in data, or open an existing data source (data file). For now click **Type in data** and then click **OK**.

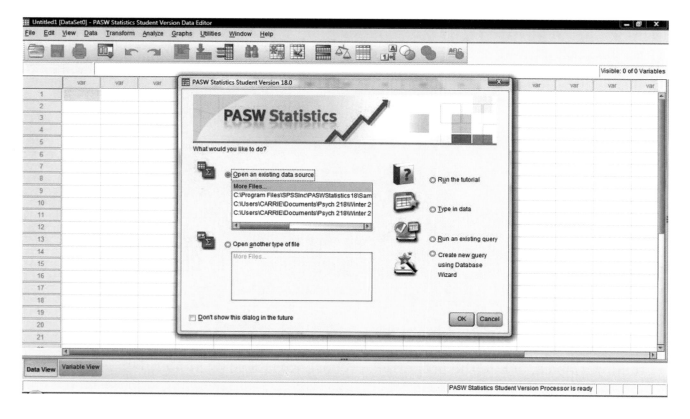

To open a data set that has been saved on your computer, click on the option to "Open an existing data source" in the dialogue box shown above and then double click the "More Files" tab to locate the data file. Alternately, you can simply double click on the file name in your computer menu. If an existing SPSS data file won't open when you double click on its file name in your computer menu, then try to first open a blank SPSS spreadsheet using the "Type in data" option. Once a blank SPSS spreadsheet is open go to File → Open → Data (or click the orange folder in the icon toolbar), locate the file on your computer, highlight the file, and then click Open.

Data and Variable View Windows

Data View

When you open SPSS it automatically displays the Data View window. As its name implies, this is where you enter the data or where the data will appear if you are opening an existing data file. Along the top of the screen you will see a toolbar with different options (e.g., File, Edit, View, Data, etc.) and another toolbar with a series of different icons.

For now let's focus on the matrix of cells occupying most of the screen. Along the top of this matrix you will see a row of cells each labeled "var" to represent variable. Along the left side of this matrix you will see a column of cells labeled with numbers. The columns in Data View represent the different variables measured. The rows in Data View represent the different subjects (or cases) assessed. Thus, any given cell represents a specific subject's score on a specific measured variable.

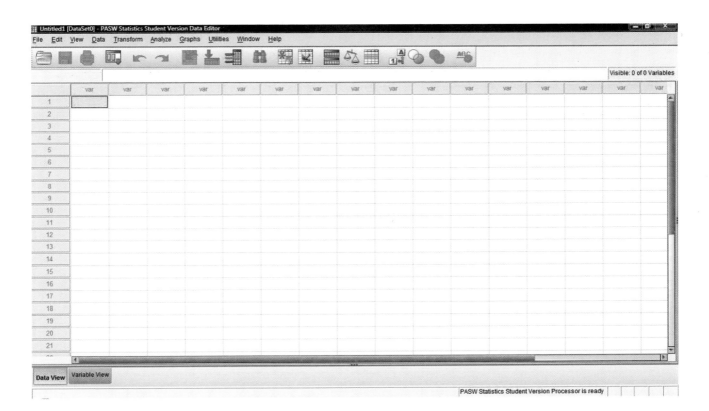

You can highlight cells in the matrix by clicking on them with your mouse or using the arrow keys. Try moving around the different cells using your mouse or arrow keys. Pressing enter will move you down one cell.

At the bottom left hand corner of the screen you will see a tab for "Data View" and a tab for "Variable View." The tab for Data View should be highlighted yellow right now because you are looking at the Data View window. Click the **Variable View** tab to open the Variable View window. It will now appear yellow.

Variable View

This window is where you go to enter in the names of your variables and to define the properties of those variables. Once entered, the variable names will appear in the top row of the Data View window in place of "var." While in Variable View you can enter the different variable names in the first column and their properties in the remaining columns. Note that the display in Variable View is opposite to the one in Data View, which shows the variable names in the top <u>row</u>.

The column labeled "Name" is where you can enter the names of your variables. The column labeled "Type" is where you can indicate the type of data you will enter (e.g., numbers, currency, strings). The column labeled "Width" is where you can set the maximum number of characters that the values of the variables can contain. The column labeled "Decimals" is where you can set the number of decimal places you want displayed for the values of the variables. The column labeled "Label" is where you can enter text descriptions of the variables. The column labeled "Values" is where you can define codes you are using to identify the values of the variables. Finally, the column labeled "Measure" is where you can specify the scales of measure used to measure the variables. Note: interval and ratio scales are both referred to as "Scale" by SPSS.

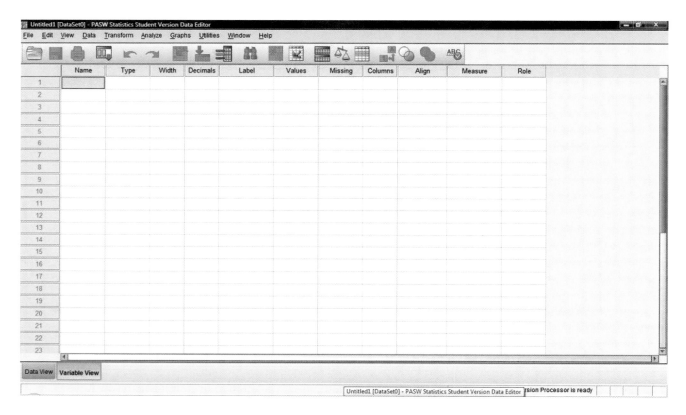

Creating Variables (in Variable View)

Let's get started by trying to create some variables. While you are in the Variable View window, type **SubjectID** in the first cell under the **Name** column (the cell that is highlighted yellow in the image displayed above). Variable names must be one word, spaces and special characters like "/" and "-" are not allowed. The subject ID codes we will be entering later to identify our subjects will contain letters and numbers. By default, SPSS only permits numbers to be entered in the Data View spreadsheet. To change this default setting you need to click on the first cell under the **Type** column. The word "Numeric" and a little blue box with three dots will then appear. Click on the little **blue box**. Options to change the type of data that can be entered will now appear in a dialogue box. Click on the **String** option. Now we will be able to enter subject ID codes that contain letters and numbers rather than just numbers. While the dialogue box is still open change the **Width** from 8 to **12** and change the number of **Decimals** from 2 to 0. Click **OK** to close the dialogue box. Now our Subject ID codes can be up to 12 characters long and a decimal remainder will not be displayed. You should notice that the first cell under the Width column now displays the value 12, and the first cell under the Decimals column now displays the value 0. We could have also changed these values by clicking on those cells under the "Width" and "Decimal" columns. Our variable name is quite informative, but this is not always the case so we should practice entering a label for the variable we just created. Click on the first cell under the **Label** column and type **Subject ID Codes**. Finally, since subject ID codes are measured on a nominal scale you should change the first cell under the **Measure** column to Nominal by clicking on the relevant cell and highlighting the word **Nominal**. Now, our first variable has been created and its properties have been defined!

Next, let's create a Weight variable. The values of this variable will represent the weights of each of the subjects in pounds. Type the word **Weight** into the second cell under the **Name** column (immediately under SubjectID). The weights we will enter will be in numerical format so leave the Type as Numeric. Notice the next cell over (under the Width column), is set so that the weights we enter can be 8 units wide (8 digits long) and the cell to the right of that (under the Decimals column) is set to have 2 decimals. Since the weights we will enter will be under 8 digits long, you can leave these settings as they are. To provide a meaningful description of the variable, you should type **Subjects' Weight in Pounds** in the second cell under the **Label** column. The scale of measure is set to Scale, which you may recall is the term SPSS uses for interval and ratio scales. Since weight is measured on a ratio scale, you can also leave that setting.

Let's also create a variable called Gender. Type the word **Gender** into the third cell under the **Name** column (immediately under Weight). We will use numerical codes to represent the different genders so you should leave Type as Numeric. Change the width of the cells to 1 by clicking on the cell under the **Width** column. Arrows should now appear. Click the **down arrow button** until it displays a value of **1**. Also change the number of decimals displayed to 0 by clicking on the cell under the **Decimal** column and then clicking the **down arrow button** until a value of 0 is displayed. To label the variable, type **Subjects' Gender** in the third cell under the **Label** column. SPSS will not analyze strings (text), so we will need to use numeric codes to label the genders. We will use 1s to designate males and 2s to designate females. To assign these numerical codes, move over to the adjacent cell in the **Values** column and click the little **blue box** that appears when the cell is highlighted. A "Value Labels" dialogue window, like the one shown on the right, should now appear. Enter a **1** in the **Value box** and **Male** in the **Label box**. Click **Add**. You just told SPSS that the Gender code 1 means male. Now enter **2** in the **Value box** and **Female** in the **Label box**. Click **Add**. Now you have told SPSS that the Gender code 2 means female. Click **OK** to close the dialogue window.

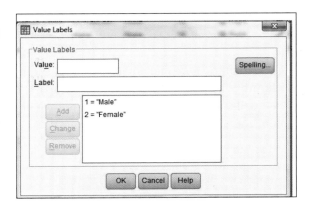

Finally, be sure to change the scale of measure to **Nominal** by clicking on the relevant cell in the **Measures** column.

Let's create one more variable. Type the word **Ethnicity** into the fourth cell under the **Name** column (immediately under Gender). We will use text to enter in the different ethnicities so change **Type** to **String**. Change the width of the cells to 9 by clicking on the cell under the **Width** column and then clicking the **up arrow button** until it displays a value of **9**. Since we have defined the variable as a String variable, the number of decimals is automatically set to 0. To label the variable, type **Subjects' Ethnicity** in the third cell under the **Label** column. Since we will be using text rather than codes to enter subjects' ethnicities, there is no need to define the values of the variables. Finally, be sure to change the scale of measure to **Nominal** by clicking on the relevant cell in the **Measures** column.

Your Variable View window should now look like the one shown below:

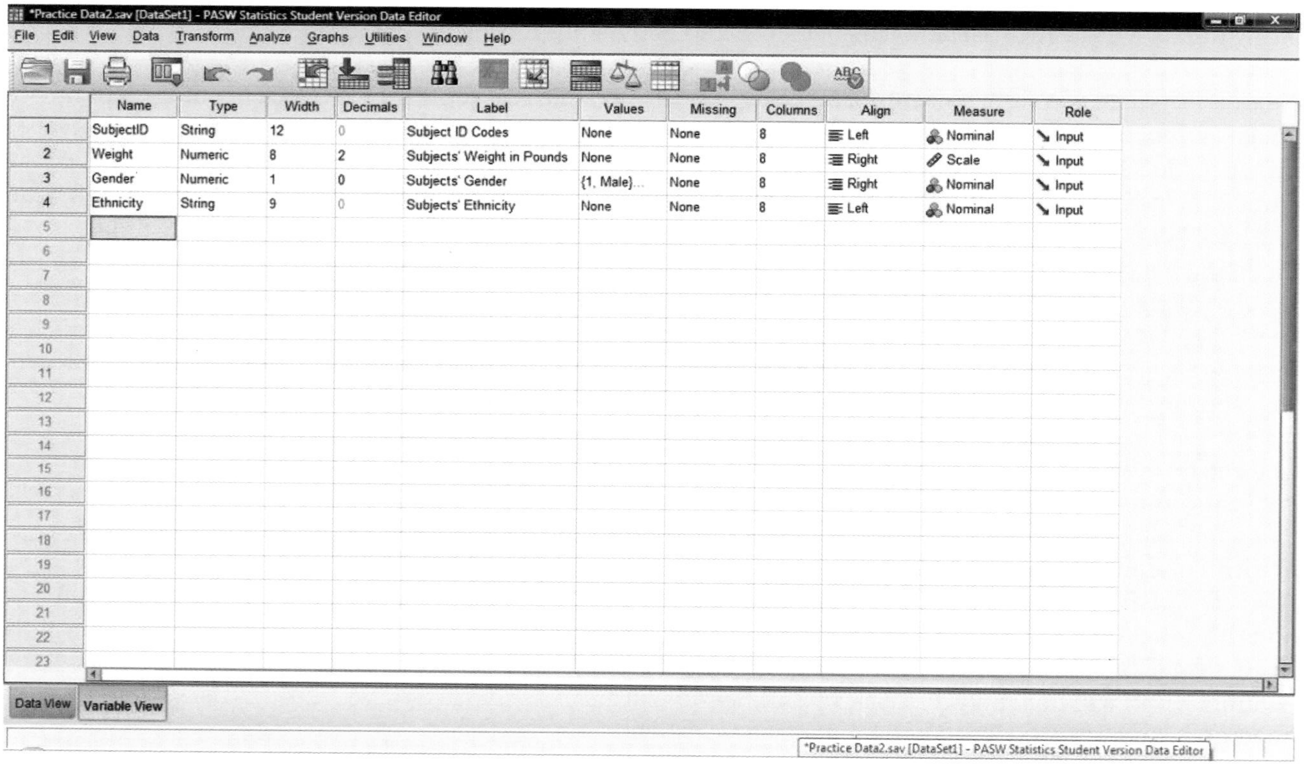

Now return to Data View by clicking on the **Data View** tab in the bottom left corner of the screen. Voilà! As highlighted in the image on the following page, you should now see that the variable names we created appear in the top row of the Data View window.

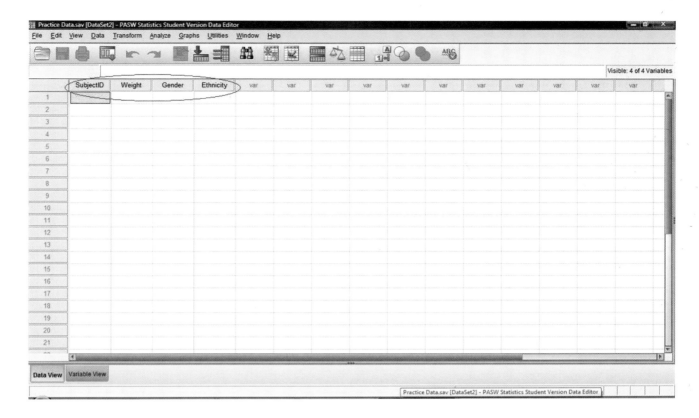

Entering Data (in Data View)

Recall that in the Data View window, each row represents a different subject's scores on the various variables. As such, we will need to enter each subject's ID code into the 1st column, each subject's weight into the 2nd column, each subject's gender code into the 3rd column, and each subject's ethnicity into the 4th column. Try entering the following data into the spreadsheet by clicking on the relevant cell and typing the information. Do not enter the variable names shown below in pink, as they should already appear in the top row of your Data View spreadsheet.

SUBJECTID	WEIGHT	GENDER	ETHNICITY
Subject1	105	2	Asian
Subject2	165	1	Caucasian
Subject3	135	2	Caucasian
Subject4	185	1	Caucasian
Subject5	120	2	Asian

Your screen should now look like the one shown on the following page. It should be clear to you by looking at the screen that the rows represent the different subjects and the columns represent the different variables. Thus, each cell represents one subject's score on one of the variables. The first subject's ID is Subject1. That subject weighs 105lbs, is female (which we coded 2) and Asian. The second subject's ID is Subject2. That subject weighs 165lbs, is male (which we coded 1), and Caucasian. The third subject's ID is Subject3. She is a Caucasian female weighing 135lbs. The fourth subject's ID is Subject4. He is a Caucasian male weighing 185lbs. The last subject's ID is Subject5. She is an Asian female who weighs 120lbs.

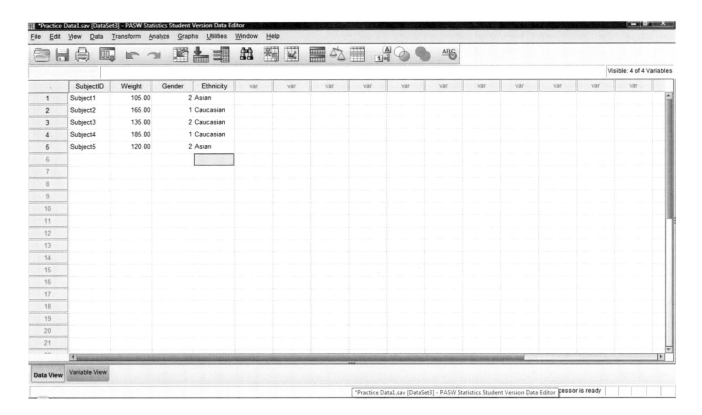

Saving the SPSS Data File (File → Save As)

Now that we've done all of this work we want to make sure we don't lose it. You can save the file by either pressing the **disk icon** in the icon toolbar or by clicking **File → Save As**. When prompted, type in the filename **Practice Data**, find a good location on your computer to save it, and press **Save**.

> Congratulations! You now know how to open SPSS, create variable names, define the properties of the variables, enter data, and save your data file. You're off to a great start!

Some Handy Tools and Tricks

Viewing Value Labels

The latest version of SPSS (Version 18) has a cool new feature that allows you to view your variable codes in the Data View window. This is useful if you forget what your codes represent, or if you are using a data file that someone else prepared and you do not know what the various codes mean. You could always check what the codes represent in the Variable View window (using the Values column), but this handy new tool allows you to see them right in the Data View window. To decode coded variables press the **Value Labels icon** in the icon toolbar. It is the icon highlighted in the image shown on the following page. To recode the variables simply press the icon again.

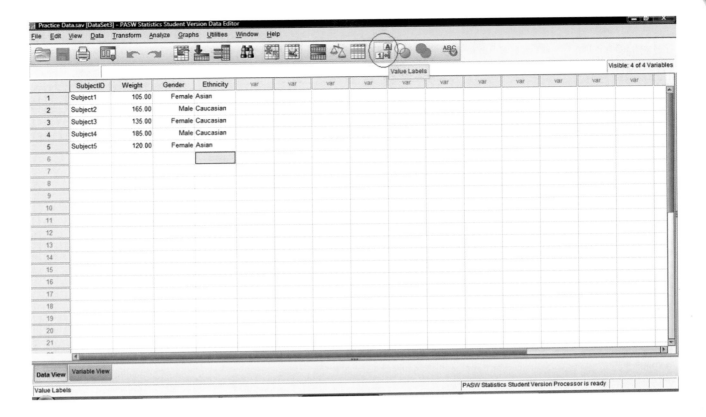

Sorting Data (Data → Sort Cases)

It is often useful to sort your data according to the values of some variable (i.e., to reorder scores from lowest to highest or highest to lowest). For instance, if we wanted to find the most extreme scores on a variable, we could sort them and then look at the scores at the very top and very bottom of the column. Let's practice using this function by sorting the data according to Weight. Go to the upper toolbar and click **Data → Sort Cases**.

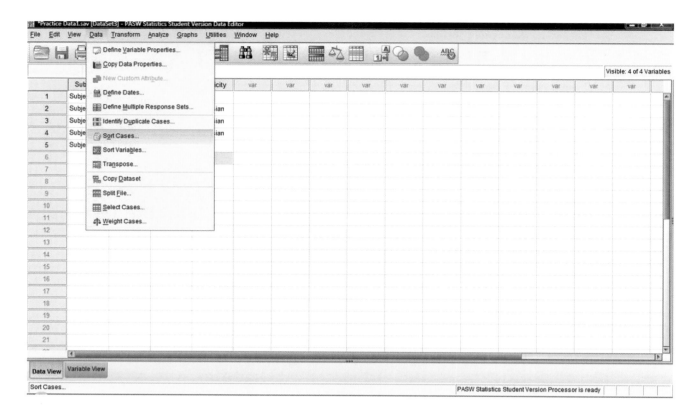

A "Sort Cases" dialogue box, like the one displayed on the right, will now appear. Highlight the **Weight** variable on the left side of the dialogue box by clicking on it, and press the **blue arrow** to move it over to the box on the right labeled, "Sort by." Notice you can choose to sort from lowest to highest (Ascending) or from highest to lowest (Descending). Leave it at the default, which is to sort in ascending order. Press **OK**.

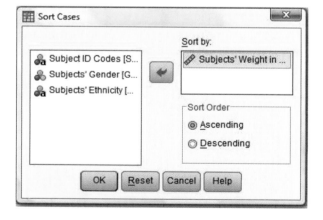

After clicking OK, you will see that the different subjects' data are organized such that the lightest subject (Subject1) is first and the heaviest subject (Subject4) is last. Try using this feature again by sorting the data back in order of SubjectID.

Selecting Cases (Data → Select Cases)

Another handy tool is selecting cases. You can think of cases as subjects. This tool allows you to perform calculations and analyses using only specific subjects' data. For instance, let's say you wanted to know the average weight of male subjects only. You would first need to select only the male subjects' data before computing the mean weight (computation of the mean is discussed in Chapter 2). To use the select cases function, go to the upper toolbar and click **Data → Select Cases**. Alternatively, you can simply click on the **Select Cases icon** in the icon toolbar. It is the icon circled in the image shown below.

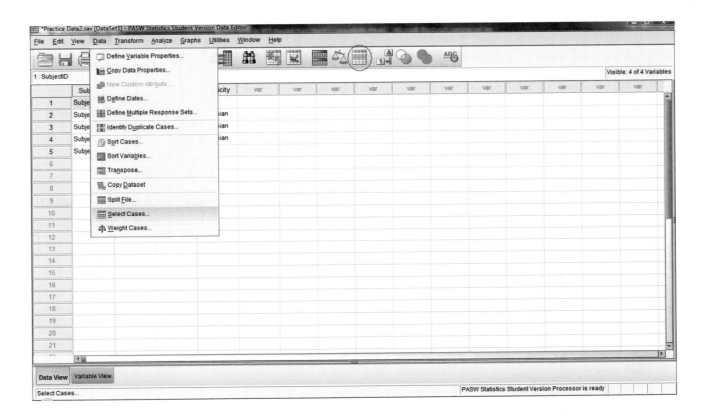

A "Select Cases" dialogue window, like the one displayed on the following page, will now appear. The default is to have all cases selected. To select only some cases, highlight **If condition is satisfied** and press the **If tab**.

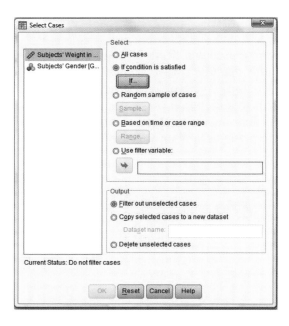

A "Select Cases: If" dialogue window, like the one shown below, will open. Highlight the **Gender** variable located on the left side of the dialogue box by clicking on it, and move it into the box on the upper right by clicking on the **blue arrow**. Next to Gender enter **= 1** using the onscreen keypad. The box should now read Gender = 1, like the one displayed below. Press **Continue** to close this dialogue box. Press **OK** to close the Select Cases dialogue box.

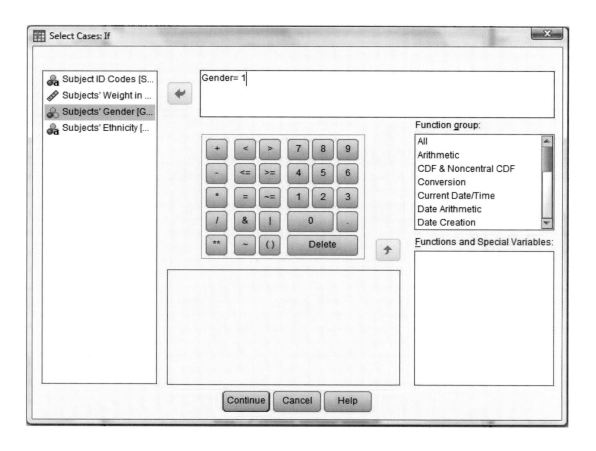

As shown in the display below, lines will now appear through the blue boxes next to Subject1, Subject3, and Subject5 (the three female subjects). The lines are indicating which subjects are being dismissed or excluded from future analyses. You should also notice a new column labeled "filter_$" has been created. The 0s in that column are indicating subjects who will be excluded from subsequent analyses because they don't meet the criteria you specified (females), and the 1s are indicating the subjects who will be included in subsequent analyses because they do meet the criteria you specified (males). Once again, you can also reveal these codes using the Value Labels icon in the icon toolbar. Rather than 1s and 0s, the words Selected and Not Selected will appear.

Note that if you wanted to do subsequent analyses on only the selected cases, you would still use the variable of interest when performing the analysis. For instance, if you wanted to calculate the mean weight of only the males, you would set the filter to select only males and then you would calculate the mean of the Weight variable. Never attempt to conduct an analysis using the "filter_$" variable as a variable. The column is only created to indicate which subjects have been filtered out; it is not a real variable and therefore should never be used in an analysis.

To reselect all cases you can simply delete the column labeled "filter_$," by right clicking on the column header (the filter_$ label) and clicking Cut. Alternatively you can click on the Select Cases icon in the icon toolbar, and then, using the "Select Cases" dialogue box, click All Cases and then press OK. Once you return to the Data View window, you will notice that the lines through the blue boxes have disappeared. Using this second option, the "filter_$" column will remain in the Data View window; however, it will now be inactive.

Next, let's try selecting subjects with weights less than or equal to 165. Click on the Select Cases icon in the icon toolbar or go to Data → Select Cases. Highlight If condition is satisfied and press the If tab.

Delete any information in the upper white box, highlight the **Weight** variable on the left side of the dialogue box by clicking on it, and move it into the upper white box on the right side by clicking on the **blue arrow**. Next to Weight enter <= **165** using the onscreen keypad (<= is designating less than or equal to). Your screen should now look like the one displayed below. Click **Continue** and then click **OK** to close the dialogue boxes.

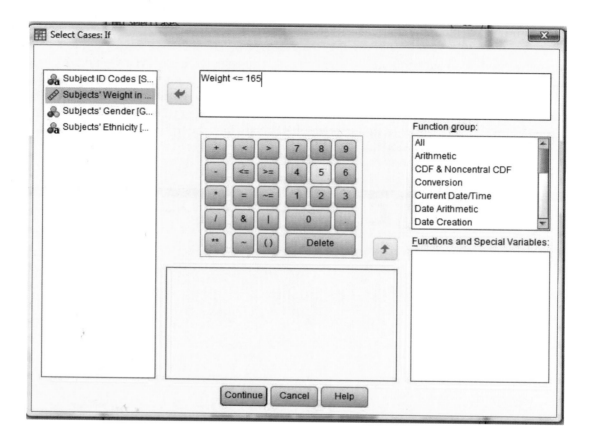

Now, the subject with a weight over 165 will not be entered into any future analyses, and your Data View window will show a line through the blue box next to his subject ID. Try reselecting all of the cases on your own so that this subject will not be excluded from our subsequent computations and analyses.

Recoding Variables (Transform → Recode into Different Variables)

Sometimes we need to recode a variable. For instance, since we entered subjects' ethnicity as a string (text) variable, we cannot perform any analyses with the variable. In order to perform analyses on this variable, we will need to recode it using numerical codes. To recode an existing variable into a different variable, go to the top toolbar and click **Transform → Recode into Different Variables**.[1]

---

[1] We could also use the option to "Recode into Same Variables," but this would overwrite our original variable.

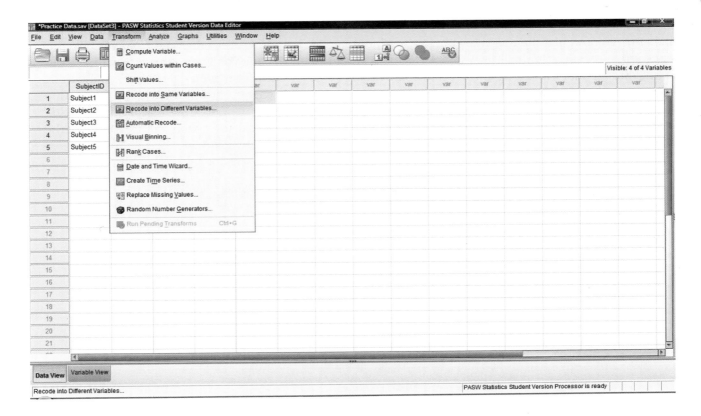

A dialogue box labeled "Recode into Different Variables," like the one shown below, will now appear. Enter the variable you want to recode—in this case **Ethnicity**—into the box labeled **String Variable →** **Output Variable**. Enter the name of the new variable you want to create—in this case **EthnicityCode**— in the box labeled **Name**. Next press **Change**.

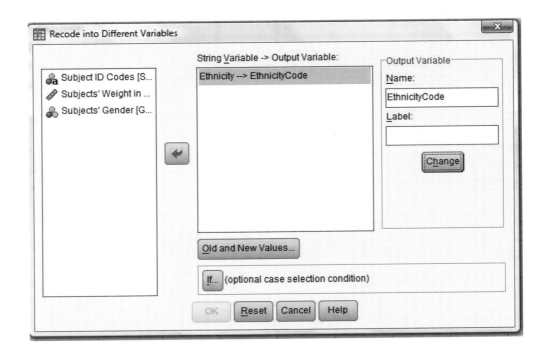

Once you have created this name for the new variable, click the tab labeled **Old and New Values**. A new dialogue window, like the one shown below, will now appear. Enter the first value of the old variable that you want to recode into the "Old Value: Value" box. Enter the new code you want to assign for that value of the variable into the "New Value: Value box." Press Add after each have been entered. Continue this process until new codes have been assigned for all of the possible values of the variable. For this example, we will recode "Caucasian" as "1" and "Asian" as "2." So you will need to enter **Caucasian** into the **Old Value: Value box** and enter a **1** into the **New Value: Value box**. Click **Add**. Next, enter Asian into the **Old Value: Value box** and enter a **2** into the **New Value: Value box**. Click **Add**.

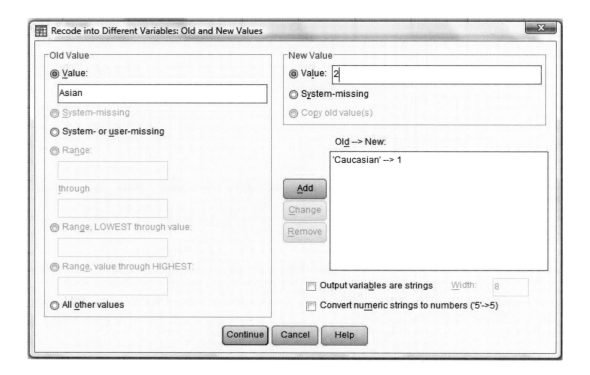

Finally, click **Continue** and then **OK** to close the dialogue boxes. As shown in the image on the following page, a new variable labeled "EthnicityCode" will now appear in the Data View window. Asian subjects are labeled with a 2 and Caucasian subjects are labeled with a 1. You should now go to the Variable View window and define the properties of this new coded variable. You should change the Width to 1 and the number of Decimals to 0. Also label the variable "Subjects' Ethnicity Coded" using the Label column, define the values of this new coded variable using the Values column, and define the scale of measure as Nominal using the Measures column (see previous section on Creating Variables if you forget how to define the properties of variables in Variable View).

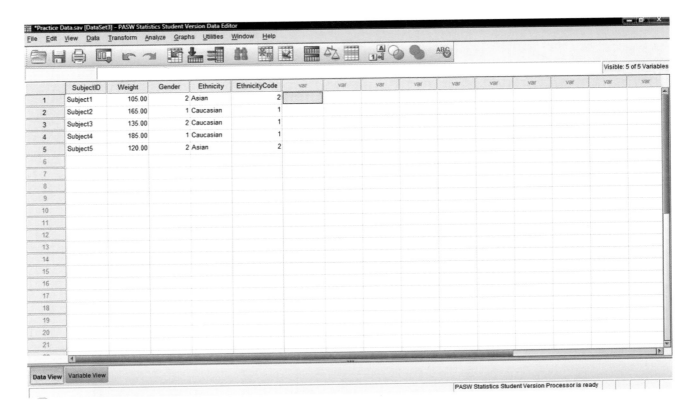

Computing New Variables (Transform → Compute Variable)

Sometimes, we need to compute a new variable from an existing variable. For instance, we may need to compute all of the subjects' weights in kilograms. To use an existing variable to compute a new variable, go to the top toolbar and click **Transform → Compute Variable**.

A "Compute Variable" dialogue window, like the one shown on the following page, will now appear. Type the name of your new variable in the **Target Variable box**. You can label the new variable **Kg**. Highlight the **Weight** variable on the left side of the dialogue box and enter it into **Numeric Expression box** on the upper right side using the **blue arrow button**. One pound equals .45 kilograms, so to convert all of the weights from pounds to kilograms, you will need to multiply each weight by .45. To do this enter *.**45** next to the variable name Weight (the "*" indicates multiplication, a "/" would indicate division). Press **OK** to close the dialogue box.

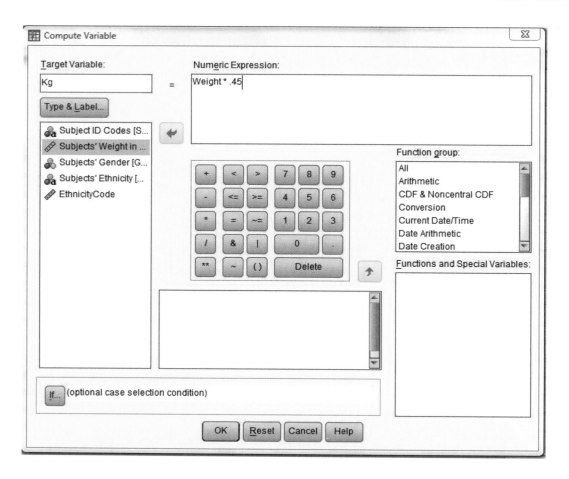

A new variable labeled Kg will now appear in your Data View window, with all of the subjects' weights in kilograms. You can do just about any mathematical transformation to your data using this handy tool!

I encourage you to explore the many handy tools and tricks available in the icon toolbar and under the Data and Transform menus in the upper toolbar. You may wish to play around with these functions on your own or by following the tutorial, which can be found using the Help menu in the upper toolbar. I suggest you create a new data file to explore functions on your own so you don't alter your practice data file.

Descriptive Statistics

2

Learning Objectives

In this chapter you will learn how to calculate indicators of central tendency (i.e., mean, median, mode) and variability (i.e., range, standard deviation, variance). You will also learn how to transform a set of raw scores to z scores.

Central Tendency and Variability

Computing the Mean, Range, Standard Deviation, and Variance

Most of the analyses you will need to conduct can be found in the upper toolbar under the "Analyze" tab. Options to calculate indicators of central tendency and variability and to analyze data using correlation, regression, t tests, and other important statistics can be found there. We'll start with computing indicators of central tendency and variability and then proceed to transforming raw scores to z scores.

With your practice data file open, use the upper toolbar to go to **Analyze** → **Descriptive Statistics** → **Descriptives**.

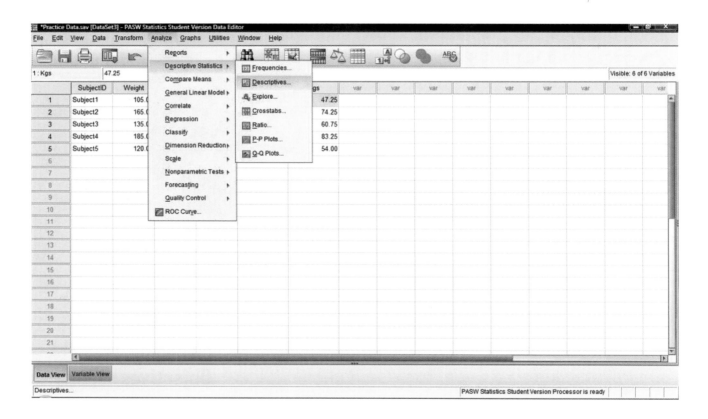

A "Descriptives" dialogue box, like the one shown on the following page, will now appear. Let's practice by requesting descriptive statistics on the variable Weight. Highlight the **Weight** variable by clicking on it and press the **blue arrow** to move it into the box labeled **Variable(s)**.

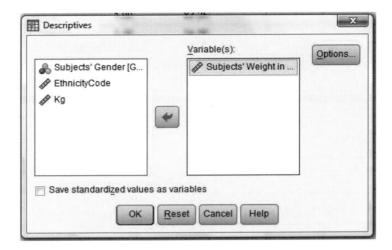

Next, click on the **Options tab**. A "Descriptives Options" dialogue box, like the one shown below, will now appear. Check the boxes next to **Mean, Std. deviation, Variance,** and **Range**. Uncheck the boxes next to **Minimum** and **Maximum**. Press **Continue** to close the dialogue box. Press **OK** to initiate the analyses.

Interpreting the Output

A new type of window called an "Output" window will now appear. Whenever you analyze data in SPSS, the results of the analyses will appear in an Output window like this one.

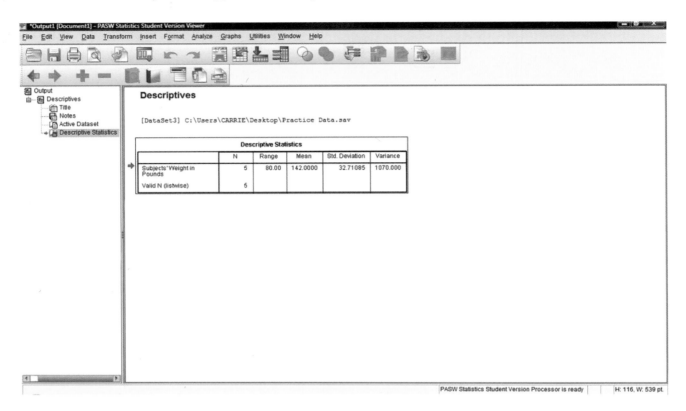

The Output window contains the "Descriptive Statistics" table shown below:

Descriptive Statistics

	N	Range	Mean	Std. Deviation	Variance
Subjects' Weight in Pounds	5	80.00	142.0000	32.71085	1070.000
Valid N (listwise)	5				

As you can see, the table shows the variable Weight and its corresponding descriptive statistics. Note, however, that since we labeled the variable, its label appears rather than the variable name. The column, labeled "N" shows the size of the sample is 5, the column labeled "Range" shows the range of weights is 80.00, the column labeled "Mean" shows the mean (i.e., average) weight is 142.00, and the column labeled "Std. Deviation" shows the standard deviation is 32.71. Finally, the column labeled "Variance" shows the variance is 1070.00. Now, that's a lot faster than hand calculations!

You might be wondering at this point why the Descriptives function doesn't contain options to calculate the median and mode. Since these statistics are less commonly used, they are hidden elsewhere. Let's go find them. Return to the Data View window by clicking the **big red star icon** in the icon toolbar in the Output window. If you are using an older version of SPSS and this icon is not available, simply minimize the Output window and maximize the Data View window using your bottom taskbar.

Computing the Median and Mode

To find the median and mode you will need to use the upper toolbar to go to **Analyze → Descriptive Statistics → Frequencies**.

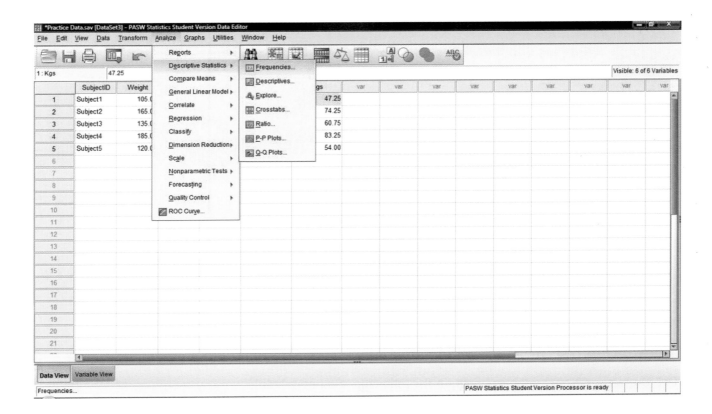

A "Frequencies" dialogue window will now open. Highlight the **Weight** variable on the left side of the box and move it into the **Variable(s) box** on the right using the **blue arrow**.

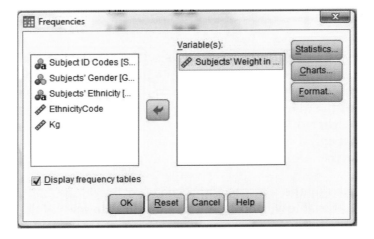

Next, press the **Statistics tab**. A "Frequencies Statistics" dialogue window, like the one shown in the image below, will now open. Check the boxes next to **Median and Mode**.

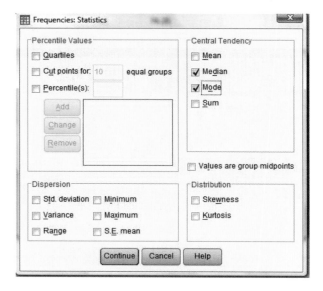

Press **Continue** and then **OK** to close the dialogue windows. If the Output window doesn't open automatically, open it by pressing the Output1 tab in your bottom taskbar.

Interpreting the Output

The Output window should now contain the following "Statistics" table:

Statistics

Subjects' Weight in Pounds

N	Valid	5
	Missing	0
Median		135.0000
Mode		105.00[a]

a. Multiple modes exist. The smallest value is shown

The first two rows provide you with the number of subjects that were included in the analysis. The 5 next to "Valid" indicates that all five subjects' data were used in the analysis. The 0 next to "Missing" means that there were data for all of the subjects on the Weight variable (i.e., we have weight data for all of the subjects). If you had deleted the weight of one subject in the Data View window before running the analysis, there would be a 1 next to Missing to indicate that one subject is missing weight data, and a 4 next to Valid to indicate that only 4 subjects' data were used in the analyses. The value of the median (135.00) is clearly shown in the third row.

Importantly, you should note that the "Statistics" table does not provide reliable information on modes. If the data contain one mode, the table will display its proper value. However, if there are multiple modes, the table will show only the lowest mode, and a note will appear under the table (like the one shown above) indicating that multiple modes exist. To find those other modes, you will need to refer to the "Frequency" table that also appears in the Output window whenever you calculate descriptive statistics using the Frequencies function.

The "Frequency" table that was produced and displayed in the Output window is presented below:

Subjects' Weights in Pounds

		Frequency	Percent	Valid Percent	Cumulative Percent
Valid	105.00	1	20.0	20.0	20.0
	120.00	1	20.0	20.0	40.0
	135.00	1	20.0	20.0	60.0
	165.00	1	20.0	20.0	80.0
	185.00	1	20.0	20.0	100.0
	Total	5	100.0	100.0	

The table clearly shows each value of the variable (each weight) in the unlabeled column. The column labeled "Frequency" shows the frequency each of the values occurred (each of the weights occurred once so 1 is listed in each cell). The column labeled "Percent" shows the relative frequency (in percentages), and the column labeled "Cumulative Percent" lists the cumulative percentages. By examining the Cumulative Percent column in the table, you should be able to determine that 80% of the subjects have a weight of 165 or lower.

When two modes exist we say the distribution is bimodal and we report both modes, but when all of the scores in a distribution have the same frequency of occurrence, we report that there is no mode. As shown above, the scores in the weight distribution all have the same frequency (a frequency of 1), so while the "Statistics" table in the Output indicates that there are multiple modes, in a case like this you would need to report that there is indeed no mode.

Transforming Raw Scores to *z* Scores

To transform a set of raw scores to *z* scores (i.e., standardized scores), use the upper toolbar to go to **Analyze → Descriptive Statistics → Descriptives**. A "Descriptives" dialogue window, like the one shown on the right, will now appear. Let's practice by transforming the weights into *z* scores. Enter **Weight** into the **Variable(s) box** by highlighting it and pressing the **blue arrow**. To obtain the *z* scores, simply check the box next to **Save standardized values as variables** in the lower left corner of the dialogue window. Press **OK**.

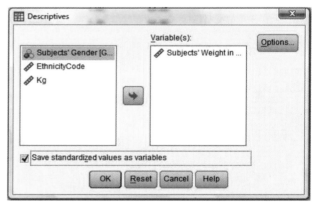

An Output window will appear showing descriptive statistics on the variable. Since we are not currently interested in these, return to the Data View window. As highlighted below, you should now see a new column of scores labeled "ZWeight." This column contains each subject's *z* score on the weight variable. For example, you can see that Subject1 received a *z* score of –1.13, indicating that she has a weight that is 1.13 standard deviations below the mean.

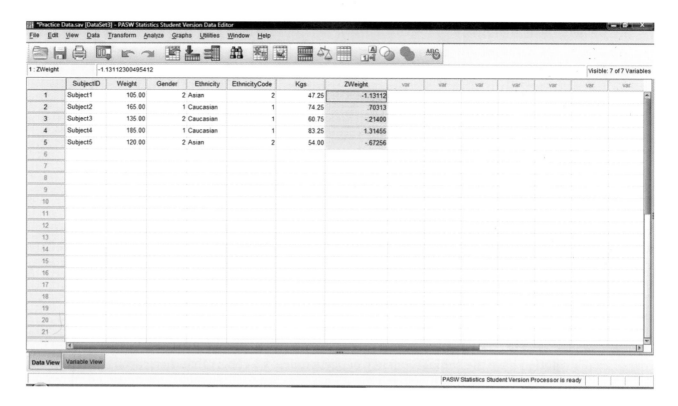

Try on Your Own

You should try combining some of the handy tools and tricks described in Chapter 1 with the analyses described in this chapter. For instance, try to find the mean weight of males and the mean weight of females (hint: select cases before running the analyses). Also try to calculate separate z scores for males and females and then use the sort cases function to find the highest z score.

Notes on Rounding

The Output window displays values rounded to various decimal places; sometimes no decimal remainders are shown, while other times five or more decimal places are given. APA style (the style of the American Psychological Association) requires us to report our results to two decimal places, so some rounding is often required. Remember: if you want to round to two decimal places and the value in the third decimal place is lower than 5, you should round down, but if the value in the third decimal place is a 5 or a value higher than 5, you should round up. When a table in the Output window shows a value rounded to 3 decimal places and the number in the third decimal place is a 5, you will need to determine if the value has been rounded up or down. To do so, simply click on the value in the table several times until the entire string of digits after the decimal place is displayed. You will then be able to make a decision about whether you need to round up or down.

Correlation

3

Learning Objectives

In this chapter you will learn how to open sample data files and create scatter plots. You will also learn how to perform and interpret the results of correlation and partial correlation analyses.

Opening a Sample Data File

SPSS comes with a large number of sample data files. For the demonstrations in this chapter, you will first need to open a sample data file entitled "Employee data." Start by opening a blank SPSS worksheet. Next, click **File → Open → Data**. Alternatively, you can simply click on the **orange folder icon** in the icon toolbar.

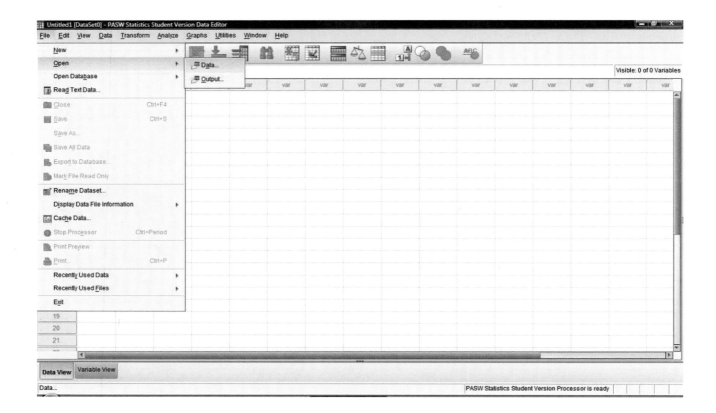

A dialogue box labeled "Open Data" will now appear. You will need to use that dialogue box to locate your SPSS files. If you followed the default installation, the SPSS program and the sample data files will be located in your Program Files. Find and open your **Program Files**, then find and open **SPSSInc → PASWStatistics18 → Samples → English**. As shown in the image on the following page, a series of sample SPSS data files should now appear. Find the file entitled **Employee data.sav** and double click on it to open it.

The Employee data file contains data on 474 subjects. Whenever you open a data file that you did not create, you should immediately examine the Variable View window to familiarize yourself with the variables, their scales, and the meaning of the values of the variables. Take a minute now to go to the **Variable View** window so you can familiarize yourself with this data file. You will see that the file contains data on each subject's gender, birth date, years of education (labeled "educ"), type of job (labeled "jobcat"), current salary in dollars (labeled "salary"), beginning salary in dollars (labeled "salbegin"), the number of months in the job (labeled " jobtime"), the number of months of previous experience (labeled "prevexp"), as well as information on whether the individual is a minority (labeled "minority").

Correlation Coefficients

Generating Scatter Plots

It is only appropriate to calculate a correlation coefficient when the variables you wish to correlate show a linear relationship. This is because the magnitude of the correlation coefficient will be underestimated if the variables show a curvilinear relationship. Thus, before conducting any correlation analysis you should first create a scatter plot to ensure that the variables show a linear relationship. To create a scatter plot you will need to use the upper toolbar to go to **Graphs → Legacy Dialogs → Scatter/Dot**.

A "Scatter/Dot" dialogue window, like the one displayed on the right, should now appear. Click on the **Simple Scatter** window and then click **Define**.

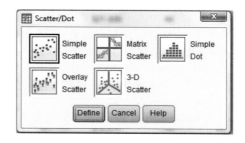

Next, a "Simple Scatterplot" dialogue window, like the one shown below, should appear. Let's create a scatter plot to examine the relationship between Current Salary and Beginning Salary. Highlight the variable **Current Salary** by clicking on it and move it over to the **Y Axis box** by clicking on the corresponding **blue arrow**. Next, highlight the variable **Beginning Salary** by clicking on it and move it over to the **X Axis box** by clicking on the corresponding **blue arrow**. Click **OK** to close the dialogue box.

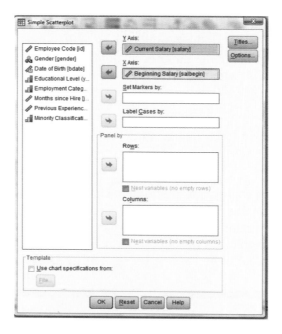

An Output window should now appear, displaying the scatter plot shown on the right. By examining the scatter plot you should be able to see that the relationship between Current Salary and Beginning Salary is clearly linear. Since the relationship is linear, it is appropriate to calculate the correlation coefficient.

Usually, scatter plots will not look quite as perfect as the one shown here. When one of the variables is nominal with two levels/values (e.g., gender), scatter plots can be particularly strange looking and difficult to interpret (the dots will all fall on two separate lines, because there are only two levels/values of the nominal variable). In most cases, you should assume the relationship is linear unless there is a clear and obvious curvilinear relationship.

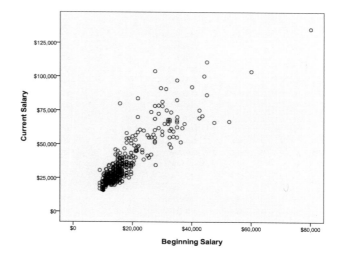

We will also correlate Education Level and Current Salary as well as Education Level and Beginning Salary, so go ahead and practice creating scatter plots for these variables as well. You will see these relationships are not nearly as clear-cut as the relationship we examined in the scatter plot depicted on the previous page. However, since there are no clear curvilinear relationships, we will proceed to compute the correlation coefficients.

Computing Correlation Coefficients

Let's start by computing the correlation coefficient for Current Salary and Beginning Salary. Using the upper toolbar, go to **Analyze → Correlate → Bivariate**.

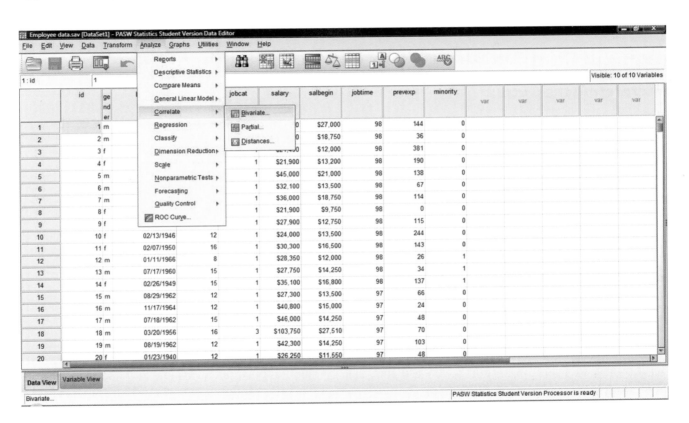

As shown in the image on the following page, a dialogue window labeled "Bivariate Correlations" should now appear with all of the variables in the data set listed on the left side.[1] Click on **Current Salary** and press the **blue arrow** to move it into the **Variables box**. Next, click on **Beginning Salary** and press the **blue arrow** to move it into the **Variables box**. Press **OK** to close the dialogue box and initiate the analysis.

---

[1] Note that the variable Gender is not contained in the list, because it was entered as a string (text) variable. SPSS will not analyze variables entered using text.

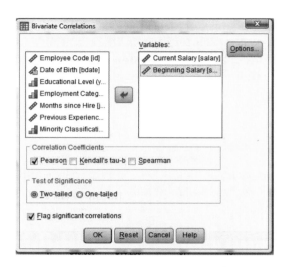

Interpreting the Output

The "Correlations" table, shown below, will now appear in the Output window:

Correlations

		Current Salary	Beginning Salary
Current Salary	Pearson Correlation	1	.880**
	Sig. (2-tailed)		.000
	N	474	474
Beginning Salary	Pearson Correlation	.880**	1
	Sig. (2-tailed)	.000	
	N	474	474

**. Correlation is significant at the 0.01 level (2-tailed).

The rows labeled "Pearson Correlation" contain the Pearson correlation coefficients. First, you should see that the correlation between Current Salary and Current Salary is 1, and that the correlation between Beginning Salary and Beginning Salary is also 1. The correlation between a variable and itself will always equal 1, so this is not terribly interesting or informative. Of primary interest, you should be able to see that the Pearson correlation between Current Salary and Beginning Salary is .88. The Pearson correlation coefficient is symbolized with an italicized r, so we can report the correlation between Beginning Salary and Current Salary in the following manner[2]: $r = .88$.

Correlation coefficients below .30 are generally interpreted as small, those between .30 and .50 are generally interpreted as moderate, and those above .50 are generally interpreted as large. Thus, our correlation of .88 indicates that there is a large positive correlation between Beginning Salary and Current Salary. We can therefore conclude that higher beginning salaries are strongly associated with higher current salaries.

---

[2] Typically, the degrees of freedom and p value are also reported along with the value of the correlation coefficient. We will review the complete style for reporting correlation coefficients in Chapter 6 when we reconsider it in the realm of inferential statistics.

The rows, in the table, labeled "N" indicate how many pairs of scores (subjects) were included in the analysis. If you were missing the beginning salary of one subject, 473 would appear in these rows rather than 474, because SPSS will only include subjects who have data on both variables.

For now, we are just focusing on correlation as a descriptive statistic (to describe the magnitude and direction of relationship between the variables). However, you should be aware that correlation can also be used in the realm of inferential statistics (to determine whether the correlation is unlikely to be due to chance, and can therefore be used to infer the magnitude and strength of the relationship in the population). We will consider correlation as an inferential statistic in Chapter 6. For now, simply note that the Correlations table shown on the previous page also contains rows labeled "Sig. (2-tailed)." The p values or significance levels provided in those rows reflect the probability that the correlation is spurious and simply due to chance. If the p value listed in the "Sig. (2-tailed)" row is less than or equal to .05, the correlation is typically regarded as being statistically significant. If the value in the "Sig. (2-tailed)" row is greater than .05, the correlation is typically regarded as not being statistically significant. The table clearly shows that the p value for the correlation between Current Salary and Beginning Salary is less than .000. Since this value is less than .05, we can conclude that there is a statistically significant correlation between the variables. The stars next to the correlation coefficients also indicate whether the correlations are significant. If there is at least one star next to the value of the correlation coefficient, it is statistically significant. If there are no stars, the correlation is not statistically significant.

Computing Correlation Coefficients with Ordinal Variables

Correlation coefficients are most commonly computed using two variables measured on interval or ratio scales. This type of correlation coefficient is referred to as a Pearson correlation coefficient, and as previously mentioned, it is symbolized as r. Correlations can also be computed with variables measured on ordinal scales. When one of the variables is measured on an ordinal scale and the other is measured on an ordinal, interval, or ratio scale, the correlation is referred to as a Spearman rank order correlation coefficient (or Spearman's rho) and it is symbolized as r_s.

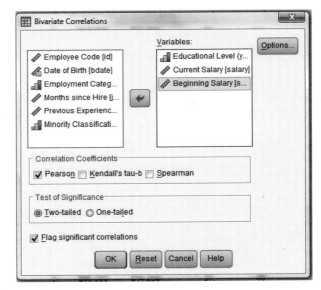

Let's begin by computing some Spearman rank order correlations using Education Level, which has been defined as an ordinal variable in this data set (see Variable View). We will correlate Education Level with Beginning Salary and Current Salary. Go to **Analyze** → **Correlate** → **Bivariate**. Put **Education Level, Current Salary**, and **Beginning Salary** in the **Variables box** by highlighting each and clicking on the blue arrow. Click **OK** to initiate the analyses.

Important Note: While the option to calculate Spearman's rho is provided in the "Bivariate Correlations" dialogue window, you should only use it if *both* of the variables you want to correlate were measured on ordinal scales. The formula for calculating Spearman's rho is merely a simplified version of Pearson's formula for ranked data. If there are no ties on the ordinal variables, then the value of

Spearman's rho will be identical to value of the Pearson correlation coefficient. However, if there are a lot of ties on the ordinal variables (and they are not handled properly), then the values of the two coefficients will be slightly different. Ties on ordinal variables should be handled in a specific way, by assigning the mean rank of the tied variables (e.g., if there is a tie for the rank of 2, both rankings should be changed to 2.5, and the ranking of 3 should be skipped). When the option to calculate Spearman's rho is checked, SPSS automatically rank orders the data and calculates and uses the mean of any tied ranks for *both* of the variables (rather than just the one defined as ordinal). For this reason, you should never use the option to calculate Spearman's rho unless both of the variables you are correlating were measured on ordinal scales. Even when both of the variables were measured on ordinal scales, the value of the Pearson correlation coefficient will be very similar to the value of Spearman's rho (and it will be identical if ties were handled properly).[3] As such, many researchers still use the option to calculate the Pearson correlation coefficient between two ordinal variables.

Interpreting the Output

The following table should now appear in the Output window. You should be able to see the correlation between Current Salary and Education Level (r_s = .66) and the correlation between Beginning Salary and Education Level (r_s = .63). These correlations indicate that there is a large positive correlation between Education Level and Current Salary, and similarly that there is a large positive correlation between Education Level and Beginning Salary. Since higher values of the variable Education Level indicate higher levels of education, we can conclude that higher levels of education are strongly associated with higher current salaries and higher beginning salaries.

Correlations

		Current Salary	Beginning Salary	Educational Level (years)
Current Salary	Pearson Correlation	1	.880[**]	.661[**]
	Sig. (2-tailed)		.000	.000
	N	474	474	474
Beginning Salary	Pearson Correlation	.880[**]	1	.633[**]
	Sig. (2-tailed)	.000		.000
	N	474	474	474
Educational Level (years)	Pearson Correlation	.661[**]	.633[**]	1
	Sig. (2-tailed)	.000	.000	
	N	474	474	474

**. Correlation is significant at the 0.01 level (2-tailed).

---

[3] You may notice that ties in the Education Level variable have not been properly handled in this data set. The option to properly rank order the data is available in SPSS (**Transform → Rank Cases**). Since it has a very small effect on the magnitude of the correlation coefficients (properly ranking the data increases each correlation by less than .02), we will not worry about ranking the data.

Computing Correlation Coefficients with Nominal Variables

Correlations can also be computed with variables measured on nominal scales as long as the nominal variables are dichotomous (they contain only two categories). Correlations should not be computed with variables measured on nominal scales that contain more than two categories, because the results would be meaningless. When one variable is measured on an interval or ratio scale, and the other is measured on a nominal scale, the correlation is referred to as a Point Biserial correlation, and it is symbolized as r_{pb}. When both of the variables are measured on nominal scales, the correlation is referred to as a Phi coefficient, and it is symbolized as ϕ.

Let's try to compute the Point Biserial correlations between Gender, Current Salary, and Beginning Salary. Since Gender is entered as a string (text) variable, we will not be able to perform any analyses with it until it is recoded using a numeric code. Go to **Transform → Recode into Different Variables**.

Label the recoded variable **GenderCode** and then proceed to recode the current gender code "**m**" to "**1**" and "**f**" to "**2**" (see the section on Recoding Variables in the Handy Tools and Tricks section of Chapter 1 if you forget how to do this). You may wish to save this data file with the recoded gender variable, as we will use this numerically recoded variable again in Chapter 4.

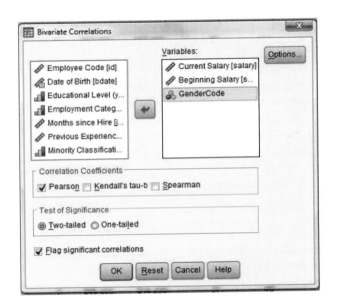

Now that we have a numerically coded gender variable, we can compute correlations with it. Point Biserial correlations and Phi coefficients are computed in the same way as Pearson correlation coefficients.[4] So using the upper toolbar, simply go to **Analyze → Correlate → Bivariate**. Enter **Current Salary, Beginning Salary**, and **GenderCode** in the **Variables** box by highlighting each and clicking on the **blue arrow**. Click **OK** to initiate the analyses.

Interpreting the Output

The "Correlations" table shown on the following page will now appear in the Output window. It clearly shows the correlation between the coded gender variable and Current Salary (r_{pb} = –.45) and the correlation between the coded gender variable and Beginning Salary (r_{pb} = –.46). These correlations indicate that there is a moderate negative correlation between GenderCode and each of Current Salary and Beginning Salary. Before we can interpret these correlations, we need to consider the code used for the gender variable. We assigned males a code of 1 (a lower value) and females a code of 2 (a higher value). The negative coefficients indicate that high values on one variable are associated with low values on the other variable. As such, we can conclude that being female is associated with lower beginning salaries and lower current salaries, or similarly, that being male is associated with higher beginning salaries and higher current salaries.

---

[4] While there are different formulas for calculating Point Biserial and Phi coefficients, they are once again merely simplified versions of Pearson's formula and they produce the same results. Since SPSS is doing all of our work we don't need to worry about simplified formulas!

Correlations

		Current Salary	Beginning Salary	GenderCode
Current Salary	Pearson Correlation	1	.880**	-.450**
	Sig. (2-tailed)		.000	.000
	N	474	474	474
Beginning Salary	Pearson Correlation	.880**	1	-.457**
	Sig. (2-tailed)	.000		.000
	N	474	474	474
GenderCode	Pearson Correlation	-.450**	-.457**	1
	Sig. (2-tailed)	.000	.000	
	N	474	474	474

**Correlation is significant at the 0.01 level (2-tailed).

Partial Correlation

Correlation does not permit determination of causation. One reason why we can never infer causation based on the results of correlation is what is referred to as the third variable problem. A correlation between two variables may appear simply because both of the variables are related to some extraneous third variable. For instance, if we discovered a correlation coefficient of −.65 (i.e., $r = -.65$) between peoples' levels of depression and the number of hours per week they spend exercising, we could not conclude based on that correlation that exercise causes people to be less depressed, or that depression causes people to exercise less, because a third variable may be responsible for the relationship. In this case, depression may be associated with reduced motivation, and reduced motivation may be associated with less exercise rather than there being a direct causal relationship between exercise and depression.

The only way to determine causality is through the use of the experimental method, because extraneous variables can be physically controlled. While we cannot physically control for extraneous variables using correlation we can statistically control for them. We can rule out third variables using a technique called partial correlation. This technique allows us to examine the relationship between two variables (e.g., exercise and depression) after statistically controlling for a potential third variable (e.g., motivation).

The partial correlation coefficient is symbolized by $r_{12.3}$. The subscripts 1 and 2 refer to the two variables you are correlating, and the subscript .3 refers to the variable you are partialling out or controlling for. For this example, the subscripts 1 and 2 refer to depression levels and hours spent exercising, and the .3 refers to motivation levels.

Interpreting Partial Correlations

Interpreting a partial correlation simply involves comparing the magnitude of the original Pearson correlation coefficient with the magnitude of the partial correlation coefficient. When the original Pearson correlation coefficient is high enough to be significant, and the partial correlation coefficient is substantially lower and is not significant, it suggests that the variable that was statistically partialed out is a third variable. In other words, if controlling for a potential third variable dramatically reduces (or eliminates) the original correlation, it suggest that the variable being controlled was responsible for the original correlation. To illustrate, assume you ran a correlation analysis and found that the correlation between depression and exercise was –.65 (r = –.65), and that it was statistically significant. Now, assume you ran a partial correlation analysis—correlating depression with exercise, after controlling for motivation—and found that the partial correlation was –.09 ($r_{12.3}$ = –.09), and that it was no longer statistically significant. Based on the difference between these coefficients, you could conclude that motivation is a third variable, and that it is responsible for the correlation between exercise and depression. The correlation between these variables was originally –.65, and it dropped substantially to –.09 after controlling for motivation, suggesting that there is little to no relationship between hours spent exercising and depression levels when motivation is statistically controlled.

When the Pearson correlation coefficient and partial correlation coefficient are identical or very similar, it suggests that the variable that was partialed out is NOT a third variable, that it is not responsible for the original correlation. In other words, if controlling for a potential third variable has little or no influence on the magnitude of the original correlation, it suggest that the variable is having little to no influence on the original correlation. To illustrate, if the original correlation between depression and exercise was –.65 (r = –.65) and the partial correlation was –.60 ($r_{12.3}$ = –.60) and both were statistically significant, you could conclude that motivation is *not* the underlying reason for the correlation between depression and exercise. This is because controlling for motivation had very little effect on the original correlation coefficient (–.60 is still very close to the original value of –.65).

When the partial correlation coefficient is significant but much lower than the original correlation coefficient, it suggests that the variable that was partialed out is a third variable, but that there is also a relationship between the variables of interest that is independent of the third variable. In other words, if a significant relationship still exists between the variables after the potential third variable is controlled, it suggests that a relationship exists between the variables of interest that is independent of the variable that was controlled. However, because controlling for the potential third variable reduced the magnitude of the original correlation, it suggests that the third variable was increasing the magnitude of the original correlation. For example, if the original correlation between depression and exercise was –.65 (r = –.65) and the partial correlation was –.45 ($r_{12.3}$ = –.45) and both were statistically significant, you would know that motivation accounts for *some* of the relationship between exercise and depression (because controlling for motivation decreased the correlation coefficient by .20), but that there is still a relationship between the depression and exercise that is independent from motivation (a correlation of –.45 is still moderately high).

Computing Partial Correlations

Let's examine whether the correlation between Current Salary and Beginning Salary is due to Education Level. In other words, let's calculate the partial correlation between Current Salary and Beginning Salary, after controlling for Education Level. Using the upper toolbar go to **Analyze → Correlate → Partial**.

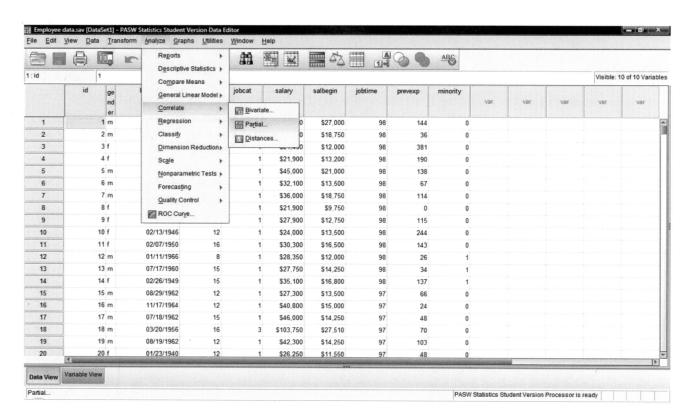

As shown below, a dialogue window labeled "Partial Correlations" should now appear. Put **Current Salary** and **Beginning Salary** in the **Variables** box using the corresponding **blue arrow**. Next, put **Education Level** in the **Controlling for** box using the corresponding **blue arrow**. Click **OK** to close the dialogue box and initiate the analysis.

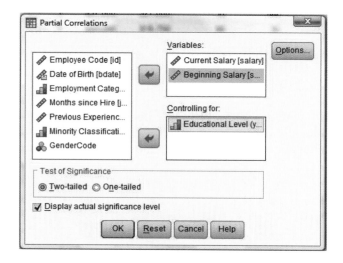

Interpreting the Output

The following "Correlations" table should now appear in the Output window:

Correlations

Control Variables			Current Salary	Beginning Salary
Educational Level (years)	Current Salary	Correlation	1.000	.795
		Significance (2-tailed)	.	.000
		Df	0	471
	Beginning Salary	Correlation	.795	1.000
		Significance (2-tailed)	.000	.
		Df	471	0

The table shows that the partial correlation between Current Salary and Beginning Salary, after controlling for Education Level, is .795. This would be reported as,[5] $r_{12.3}$ = .79. Since the significance value listed in the row labeled "Significance (2-tailed)" is less than .05, the partial correlation is statistically significant. For some reason, stars are not placed next to significant *partial* correlations, so you will need to rely on the value in this row to make a determination of statistical significance.

Now, as you may recall, the original correlation between Current Salary and Beginning Salary was .88 (r = .88), and it was statistically significant. Controlling for Education really didn't have much of an effect on the correlation between Current Salary and Beginning Salary. Based on these results, we can conclude that Education is not a third variable, that it is not responsible for the correlation between Current Salary and Beginning Salary. Indeed, we wouldn't expect education to have much of an influence on the relationship between these variables.

Next, let's try to calculate the partial correlation between Current Salary and Education Level, controlling for Beginning Salary. Go to **Analyze** → **Correlate** → **Partial**. Put **Current Salary** and **Education Level** in the **Variables box** using the corresponding **blue arrow** and put **Beginning Salary** in the **Controlling for box** using the corresponding **blue arrow**. Click **OK** to close the dialogue box and initiate the analysis.

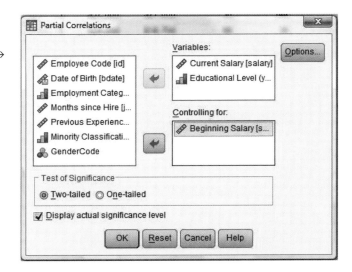

---

[5] The value that appears in the table is .795. However, as discussed at the end of Chapter 2, the value displayed in the table has been rounded to three decimal places. If you repeatedly click on the value displayed in the table, you will see that the actual value of the correlation coefficient is .7948028667407674, which we would round to .79. This is a good illustration that when there is a 5 in the 3rd decimal place, you should always click on the tabled value to avoid rounding error!

The following table will appear in your Output window:

Correlations

Control Variables			Current Salary	Educational Level (years)
Beginning Salary	Current Salary	Correlation	1.000	.281
		Significance (2-tailed)	.	.000
		Df	0	471
	Educational Level (years)	Correlation	.281	1.000
		Significance (2-tailed)	.000	.
		Df	471	0

The table shows that the partial correlation between Current Salary and Education, after controlling for Beginning Salary, is .28. We would once again report this as, $r_{12.3}$ = .28. Since the significance value is less than .05, we know that the partial correlation is statistically significant. However, partialling out Beginning Salary has caused a substantial decrease in the value of the correlation coefficient. The original correlation between Current Salary and Education Level was .66 (r_s = .66). The large reduction in the value of the partial correlation suggests that much of the correlation between Current Salary and Education Level is simply due to Beginning Salary. With that said, since the partial correlation is still significant, we know that a relationship exists between Current Salary and Education Level that is independent of Beginning Salary (it is just much smaller than the original correlation coefficient would have led us to believe). This makes sense; people with higher beginning salaries have more education and higher current salaries, inflating the correlation between Current Salary and Education.

Regression

4

Learning Objectives

In this chapter you will learn how to perform simple regression and multiple regression analyses. You will also learn how to use the results of the analyses to construct the least-squares regression line and make predictions. Finally, you will learn how to interpret the standard error of estimate and coefficient of determination.

Simple Regression

Conducting a Simple Regression Analysis

We will once again use the sample data file "Employee data" for the demonstrations in this chapter. If you saved the file used for the demonstrations in Chapter 3, you should use it (because we will once again consider the recoded gender variable). If you didn't save the file, the original one can be found in your SPSS program file (refer to the section of Chapter 3 on Opening A Sample Data File, if you forget how to do this).

We will begin with a simple (one predictor) regression analysis. Let's examine whether we can use number of years of education to predict peoples' beginning salaries. Thus, for this analysis Beginning Salary will be our Y variable (the variable we want to predict or the "criterion variable") and years of education will be our X variable (the "predictor variable"). To conduct the analysis, use the upper toolbar to go to **Analyze → Regression → Linear**.

A "Linear Regression" dialogue window, like the one shown on the right, will now open. Enter the variable you want to predict (**Beginning Salary**) into the **Dependent box** using the corresponding **blue arrow**. Next, enter the predictor variable (**Education Level**) into the **Independent(s) box** using the corresponding **blue arrow**. Click **OK**.

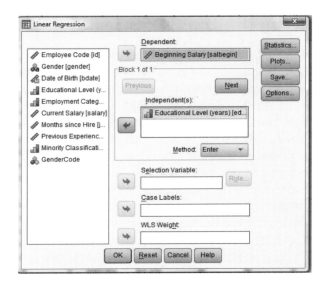

Constructing the Equation for the Least-Squares Regression Line

A number of results tables will now appear in the Output window, only two of which are meaningful for our current purposes.[1] First, scroll down to the table labeled "Coefficients" (it is the last table presented in the Output). This table contains the regression coefficients, which we need to construct the equation of the least-squares regression line. The table is shown below:

Coefficients[a]

Model		Unstandardized Coefficients		Standardized Coefficients	t	Sig.
		B	Std. Error	Beta		
1	(Constant)	-6290.967	1340.920		-4.692	.000
	Educational Level (years)	1727.528	97.197	.633	17.773	.000

The equation for the least-squares regression line is Y' = bX + a. "Y'" represents the criterion variable (the variable we want to predict), "b" represents the slope of the least-squares regression line, "X" represents the person's score on the predictor variable, and "a" represents the intercept of the least-squares regression line. The table above displays the values of the slope (b) and intercept (a) in the column labeled "B." The slope (b) is presented in the row labeled with the predictor variable; in this case it is labeled "Education Level (years)." By looking at the table you should be able to see that the slope of the least-squares regression line is 1727.528. The intercept (a) is presented in the row labeled "(Constant)." You should be able to see that the intercept is –6290.967. Now, we have all of the information we need to construct the equation for the least-squares regression line. Y' = bX + a = 1727.53X – 6290.97. You may refer to the footnote if you would like an explanation of the value listed in the column labeled Beta.[2]

---

[1] The ANOVA table provides information on the significance of the regression model. Since we are only considering regression as a descriptive statistic, it is not considered further.

[2] The value listed in the column labeled Beta provides the standardized regression coefficient, which is the slope of the least-squares regression line for the standardized (z transformed) variables. For simple regression, the value of Beta is the same as the value of the correlation coefficient. Thus, by referring to the "Coefficients" table you can see that the correlation between Beginning Salary and Education Level is, r = .63. Note that the same value is provided in the R column of the Model Summary table.

Using the Least-Squares Regression Line to Make Predictions

Now that we have constructed the equation for the least-squares regression line, we can go ahead and make predictions of peoples' beginning salaries based on their years of education. For example, what beginning salary would we predict for an individual with 16 years of education? To answer this question, all we need to do is substitute 16 (the person's score on the X variable) in for X and solve for Y'. Let's go ahead and do that, Y' = 1727.5283(16) – 6290.9673 = 21349.49. Thus, we would predict a beginning salary of $21,349.49 for a person with 16 years of education. Apparently these data are a bit out-dated; you will probably be earning more than that with your four years of postsecondary education! Note that we used values rounded to 4 decimal places (rather than 2 decimal places) when we were using the least-squares regression line to make the prediction in order to increase the accuracy of our prediction, and we only rounded the final predicted value to 2 decimal places. While the SPSS output only displays 3 decimal places, the remaining decimal places can be revealed by repeatedly clicking on the value in the table in the Output window.

Determining the Standard Error of Estimate

Now, how much confidence should we have in our predictions? How much error will our predictions contain? To answer these questions, we need to consider the standard error of estimate. The standard error of estimate provides an indicator of the average amount of error that we can expect in our predictions. The standard error of estimate can be found in the table labeled "Model Summary" (the second table presented in the Output window) in the column labeled "Std. Error of the Estimate." The table is presented below:

Model Summary

Model	R	R Square	Adjusted R Square	Std. Error of the Estimate
1	.633[a]	.401	.400	$6,098.259

a. Predictors: (Constant), Educational Level (years)

A quick glance at this table reveals that the standard error of estimate is $6,098.259. This value means that on average we can expect our predictions of peoples' beginning salaries to be off by about $6,098.26.

Bivariate Correlation and the Coefficient of Determination (r^2)

The "Model Summary" table shown above contains additional useful information, including the correlation between the X and Y variables (Education Level and Beginning Salary) and the coefficient of determination. The column labeled "R" shows that the correlation between the two variables is .633. Since we are using simple rather than multiple regression (i.e., we have only one predictor variable), the capitalized R should really be a lower case r, but sometimes SPSS doesn't make these subtle distinctions. Thus, we would report this correlation as, r_s = .63.

The coefficient of determination (r^2) is presented in the column labeled "R Square" (once again the capitalized R should really be a lower case r because we only have one predictor variable). The table clearly shows that coefficient of determination is .401, which we would report as r^2 = .40. This means that

40.09% (.4009 x 100) of the variability of Y (Beginning Salary) is accounted for by X (Education Level). In other words, 59.91% of the variability in beginning salaries is still not accounted for (we don't know where it comes from). Note that we used values rounded to 4 decimal places (rather than 2 decimal places) when we were using the coefficient of determination to determine the percentage of variability of Y accounted for by X, so that the value is accurate to 2 decimal places. Once again, while the SPSS output only displays 3 decimal places, the remaining decimal places can be revealed by repeatedly clicking on the value in the table in the Output window.

The table also displays the Adjusted R Square. For simple regression, the value of the adjusted r^2 will always be nearly identical to the value of r^2. You will notice bigger differences between the adjusted R^2 and R^2 as you add more predictor variables in multiple regression analyses. While R^2 will almost always increase as you add more predictor variables (so long as they are correlated with the criterion), adjusted R^2 adjusts for the number of predictors used, and only increases if a predictor improves the prediction more than would be expected based on chance.

Multiple Regression with Two Predictors

In this next section you will learn how to perform a multiple regression analysis. Multiple regression is simply an extension of simple regression. Simple regression is used to make predictions on the basis of one variable, while multiple regression is used to make predictions using more than one predictor variable. We will begin by considering multiple regression with two predictors.

Let's say we want to predict peoples' beginning salaries based on their years of education *and* their previous work experience. Now, we are in the land of multiple regression, because we are using more than one predictor variable. In this example, Beginning Salary is the variable we want to predict (the criterion variable), and it is labeled Y' just as it was in simple regression. Education Level and Previous Experience are the variables we will use to make predictions (the predictor variables). The predictor variables are labeled X as in simple regression, but now since there are two predictor variables, we need to distinguish them from each other using subscripts. Thus, we will label Education Level X_1 and Previous Experience X_2.

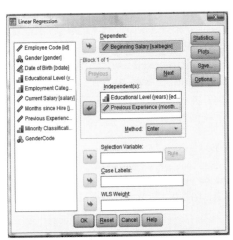

Conducting a Multiple Regression Analysis

To run the analysis, go to **Analyze → Regression → Linear**. A "Linear Regression" dialogue window, like the one shown in the adjacent image, will open. Enter the criterion variable (**Beginning Salary**) into the **Dependent box** using the corresponding **blue arrow**. Next enter the predictor variables (**Education Level**) and (**Previous Experience**) into the **Independent(s) box** using the corresponding **blue arrow**. Click **OK** to close the dialogue box and run the analysis.

Constructing the Equation for the Least-Squares Regression Line

Once again, a number of results tables will now appear in the Output window, only two of which are meaningful for our current purposes. We will start with the last table, labeled "Coefficients." It is shown on the following page:

Coefficients[a]

Model		Unstandardized Coefficients		Standardized Coefficients	T	Sig.
		B	Std. Error	Beta		
1	(Constant)	-9902.786	1417.474		-6.986	.000
	Educational Level (years)	1878.211	96.717	.688	19.420	.000
	Previous Experience (months)	16.470	2.668	.219	6.174	.000

a. Dependent Variable: Beginning Salary

The multiple regression equation for two predictor variables is $Y' = b_1X_1 + b_2X_2 + a$. Note that it is very similar to the simple regression equation ($Y' = bX + a$); it has simply been expanded to include two predictor variables (X_1 and X_2) and each of their slopes (b_1 and b_2).

The values of the intercept (a) and slopes (b_1 and b_2) are presented in the column labeled "B." The slope of each predictor variable is presented in the row labeled with the name of the predictor variable. You should be able to see that b_1 (the slope for Education Level), is 1878.211, and b_2 (the slope for Previous Experience) is 16.470. The intercept is once again presented in the row labeled "(Constant)." You should see that the value of the intercept is −9902.786. This is all of the information we need to construct the equation of the least-squares regression line. We simply need to substitute these values in for b_1, b_2, and a. Thus, $Y' = b_1X_1 + b_2X_2 + a = 1878.21X_1 + 16.47X_2 − 9902.79$.

Using the Least-Squares Regression Line to Make Predictions

Now that the equation for the regression line has been constructed, we can begin making predictions of peoples' beginning salaries based on their years of education and months of previous work experience. What beginning salary would we predict for an individual with 16 years of education and 110 months of previous experience? To answer this question, all we need to do is substitute 16 in for X_1, and 110 in for X_2, and then solve for Y'. Let's go ahead and do that. $Y' = 1878.2114(16) + 16.4704(110) − 9902.7860 = 21960.34$. Thus, we would predict a beginning salary of about $21,960.34 for a person with 16 years of education and 110 months of previous experience. Once again, please note that we used values rounded to 4 decimal places when we were using the least-squares regression line to make the prediction in order to increase the accuracy of our prediction, and we only rounded our final answer to 2 decimal places.

Determining the Standard Error of Estimate

Next, let's consider the results appearing in the "Model Summary" table presented in the Output window. The table is shown below:

Model Summary

Model	R	R Square	Adjusted R Square	Std. Error of the Estimate
1	.668[a]	.446	.443	$5,871.763

a. Predictors: (Constant), Previous Experience (months), Educational Level (years)

From a quick glance at this table you should be able to see that the standard error of estimate is $5,871.763. This means that on average we can expect our predictions of peoples' beginning salaries to be off by about $5,871.76. You should note that adding previous experience as a second predictor variable reduced the error in our predictions from $6,098.26 (as shown in the Model Summary table in the Simple Regression section) to $5,871.76. In other words, our prediction accuracy was improved by adding the second predictor variable, previous experience.

Multiple Correlation and the Coefficient of Determination (R^2)

The Model Summary table also shows that the Multiple Correlation is .668, which we would report as, R = .67. Now that we have multiple predictors (i.e., X variables), it is appropriate to use a capitalized R. By repeatedly clicking on the value listed in the column labeled "R Square" you will see that the Multiple Coefficient of Determination is .4458 (R^2 = .45). From this we can conclude that 44.58% (.4458 × 100) of the variability of beginning salaries can be accounted for (or explained by) years of education and months of previous experience. That means that 55.42% of the variability in beginning salaries is still not accounted for (we don't know where it comes from). If you'll recall we were able to account for 40.09% of the variability when we were using only Education Level as a predictor variable. Thus, by adding in Previous Experience as a second predictor variable we are able to account for more of the variability in Beginning Salary.

Multiple Regression with Three Predictor Variables

The multiple regression equation for three predictor variables is: $Y' = b_1X_1 + b_2X_2 + b_3X_3 + a$. Note that it is very similar to the multiple regression equation for two predictor variables ($Y' = b_1X_1 + b_2X_2 + a$.); it has simply been expanded to include a third predictor variable (X_3) and its slope (b_3).

To illustrate multiple regression with three predictor variables (one of which is a nominal variable with 2 categories), let's try to predict Current Salary using Education Level, Previous Experience, and Gender. We will label Education Level X_1, Previous Experience X_2, and Gender X_3.

Since Gender was originally entered as a string (text) variable, we will not be able to perform any analyses with it until it is recoded using a numeric code. If you are not using the data file you used in Chapter 3 with the numerically recoded Gender variable, then you will need to recode the Gender variable. To do so, go to **Transform → Recode into Different Variables**. Label the recoded variable **GenderCode** and then proceed to recode the current gender code "**m**" to "**1**" and "**f**" to "**2**." (see the section on Recoding Variables in the Handy Tools and Tricks section of Chapter 1 if you forget how to do this).

Conducting a Multiple Regression Analysis

Go to **Analyze → Regression → Linear**. Using the "Linear Regression" dialogue window shown on the following page enter the criterion variable, the variable we want to predict (**Beginning Salary**), into the **Dependent box** using the corresponding **blue arrow**. Next, enter all three predictor variables (**Education Level**), (**Previous Experience**), and (**Gender**) into the **Independent(s) box** using the corresponding **blue arrow**. Click **OK** to close the dialogue window and initiate the analysis.

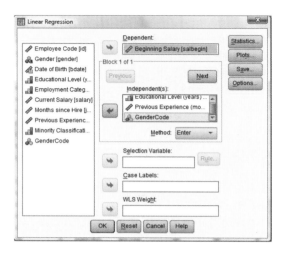

Constructing the Equation for the Least-Squares Regression Line

The following table will now appear in your Output window:

Coefficients[a]

Model		Unstandardized Coefficients		Standardized Coefficients	T	Sig.
		B	Std. Error	Beta		
1	(Constant)	-1045.042	2030.198		-.515	.607
	Educational Level (years)	1625.292	102.753	.596	15.817	.000
	Previous Experience (months)	12.001	2.685	.159	4.469	.000
	GenderCode	-3446.504	583.307	-.218	-5.909	.000

a. Dependent Variable: Beginning Salary

Let's first find the values of the slopes and intercept. Once again, they are all presented in the column labeled "B." By looking at the table you should be able to see that b_1 (the slope for Education Level), is 1625.292, b_2 (the slope for Previous Experience) is 12.001, and b_3 (the slope for GenderCode) is –3446.504. The negative value of b_3 indicates that the slope for our coded gender variable is an inverse slope. In other words, the negative value of b_3 means that the relationship between the predictor variable and the criterion variable is negative (that as the value of the predictor variable increases, the value of the criterion variable decreases). Since gender is a nominal variable and we used numeric codes to represent the values of this variable, we need to carefully consider the codes that we used before we can understand the nature of this relationship. If you'll recall, we used a code of 1 to represent the male gender and a code of 2 to represent the female gender. As such, the negative slope associated with this variable indicates that being female (a higher value) is associated with lower beginning salaries, and similarly, that being male (a lower value) is associated with higher beginning salaries. The intercept is once again presented in the row labeled "(Constant)," it is –1045.042. We now have all of the information we need to construct the equation of our regression line: all we need to do is substitute in the values of b_1, b_2, b_3, and a. $Y' = b_1X_1 + b_2X_2 + b_3X_3 + a = 1625.29X_1 + 12.00X_2 - 3446.50X_3 - 1045.04$.

Using the Least-Squares Regression Line to Make Predictions

Now that we have our regression equation we can use it to predict peoples' beginning salaries based on their years of education, months of previous experience, and gender. Let's say that Joe (a male) has 16 years of education and 110 months of previous experience. What would we predict his beginning salary to be? To answer this question, we simply need to substitute these values into the corresponding X values in our regression equation and then solve the equation. Since we labeled Education Level X_1, Previous Experience X_2, and GenderCode X_3, we need to substitute 16 in for X_1, 110 in for X_2, and 1 (the numeric code we have assigned for males) in for X_3. Let's go ahead and do that. $1625.2918(16) + 12.0014(110)$ $- 3446.5036(1) - 1045.0423$. Now we are ready to solve the equation, $Y' = 26004.6688 + 1320.1540$ $- 3446.5036 - 1045.0423 = 22,833.2769$. Thus, we would predict Joe's current salary to be about $22,833.28. Try to predict what Jane's (a female) current salary would be if she has the same number of years of education and months of previous experience as Joe.

Determining the Standard Error of Estimate

We are now ready to consider the "Model Summary" table shown below:

Model Summary

Model	R	R Square	Adjusted R Square	Std. Error of the Estimate
1	.696[a]	.484	.481	$5,671.155

a. Predictors: (Constant), GenderCode, Previous Experience (months), Educational Level (years)

The table shows that the standard error of estimate is $5,671.55. This means that we can expect that on average our predictions of peoples' current salaries using this regression equation will be off by about $5,671.55. You should note that adding gender as a third predictor variable reduced the error in our predictions from $5,871.76 (as shown in the Model Summary table in the Multiple Regression with Two Predictors section above) to $5,671.55. In other words, our prediction accuracy was improved by adding the third predictor variable, GenderCode.

Multiple Correlation and the Coefficient of Determination (R^2)

Finally, by referring to the column labeled "R" in the "Model Summary" table, you should be able to see that the Multiple Correlation is .696, which we would report as, $R = .70$. By repeatedly clicking on the R Square value in the table, you will see that the Multiple Coefficient of Determination is .4841, which we would report as, $R^2 = .48$. Thus, 48.41% of the variability in current salary is accounted for by years of education, months of previous experience, and gender. If you'll recall, we were able to account for 44.58% of the variability when we were using only Education Level and Previous Experience as predictor variables. By adding in GenderCode as a third predictor variable, we are able to account for more of the variability in Beginning Salary.

The least-squares regression equation can be expanded to include 4, 5, or more predictors in the same way it was expanded to include 2 and 3 predictors (by adding in additional b and X terms). You can go ahead and try to build and use an equation with 4 predictors as additional practice. Try using Education Level, Previous Experience, GenderCode, and Current Salary to predict Beginning Salary.

Sign Test

5

In this chapter you will learn how to analyze data using the sign test. You will learn how to conduct the analysis and interpret the results for both two-tailed and one-tailed tests.

Non-Directional Hypotheses and Two-Tailed Sign Tests

Imagine you have just been hired by a market research firm to conduct a Pepsi Challenge in order to determine whether students on your campus prefer the taste of Pepsi or Coke. Your alternative hypothesis (H_1) is that the two brands of pop will not be equally preferred (i.e., that one brand will be preferred over the other). Accordingly, your null hypothesis (H_0) is that the two brands of pop will be equally preferred (i.e., that one brand will not be preferred over the other). Prior to conducting the experiment, you decide to stick with convention and set alpha at .05 (meaning you are willing to accept a 5% chance that you will make an incorrect decision to reject the null hypothesis).

Assume that you decide to use a repeated measures design.[1] You go to the Student Union Building and ask 12 students to do a blind taste test. Each student is asked to take a sip of Pepsi and a sip of Coke and then to indicate which they prefer. To guard against order effects you use complete counterbalancing. You randomly select 6 students to take a sip of Pepsi first and a sip of Coke second, and 6 students to take a sip of Coke first and a sip of Pepsi second.

Assume you obtain the results shown below. A "1" indicates that the subject preferred the soft drink and a "2" means they didn't prefer the soft drink. You should be able to see that Subject 1 preferred Pepsi while Subject 4 preferred Coke.

SUBJECTID	COKE	PEPSI
1	2	1
2	2	1
3	2	1
4	1	2
5	2	1
6	2	1
7	2	1
8	1	2
9	2	1
10	2	1
11	2	1
12	2	1

Begin by opening SPSS and entering in the data. Note that the top row contains the variable names that must be entered in the Variable View window (see Chapter 1). While you are in Variable View, you should label the values of the variables using the "Values" column: Label "1" as "Preferred" and "2" as "Not Preferred," and define the scale of measure as "Nominal." The data in the remaining rows must be entered in Data View (see Chapter 1). Once the data are entered, your Data View window should look like the one shown on the following page:

---

[1] The sign test requires the use of a repeated measures (i.e., within-subject) design.

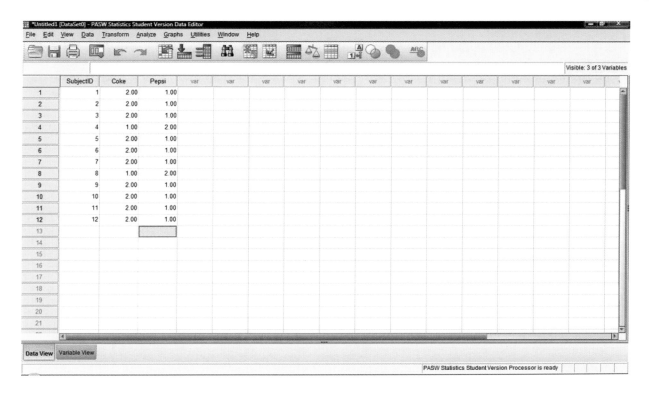

Conducting the Sign Test Analysis

To initiate the sign test analysis, use the upper toolbar to go to **Analyze → Nonparametric Tests → Legacy Dialogs → 2 Related Samples.**[2]

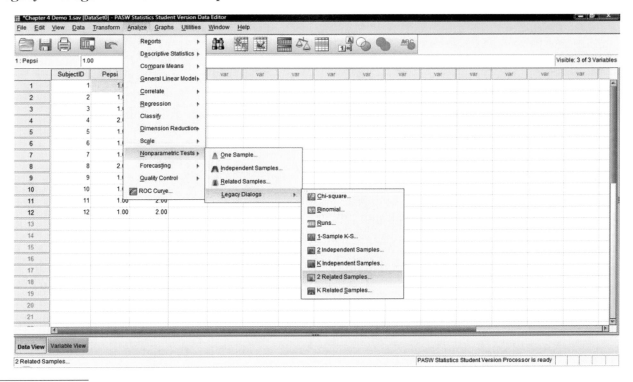

---

[2] In previous versions of the software the sign test option was under **Analyze → Nonparametric Tests → 2 Related Samples.**

A dialogue window labeled "Two-Related-Samples Tests" should now appear with the variables listed on the left side. Highlight the relevant variables—**Pepsi** and **Coke**—by simply clicking on each variable once and move the pair over to the **Test Pairs box** by clicking on the **blue arrow. Check** the box labeled **Sign** and **uncheck** the box labeled **Wilcoxon.** Click **OK** to close the dialogue window and execute the analysis.

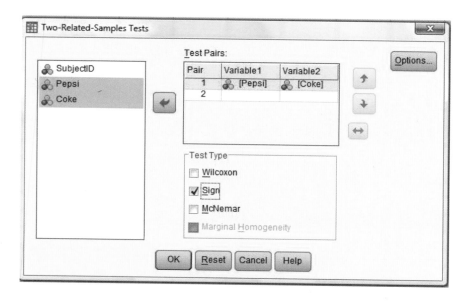

Interpreting the Output

An Output window should now appear displaying two tables. Let's begin by examining the "Frequencies" table shown below:

Frequencies		N
Coke – Pepsi	Negative Differences[a]	2
	Positive Differences[b]	10
	Ties[c]	0
	Total	12

a. Coke < Pepsi

b. Coke > Pepsi

c. Coke = Pepsi

The "Frequencies" table displays the total number of negative differences (– signs), the total number of positive differences (+ signs), and the total number of ties. Since the signs are arbitrary and meaningless unless you know which variable was subtracted from which, the superscripts a, b, and c presented in the table are useful for clarifying what a negative difference represents, what a positive difference represents, and what a tie represents. By looking at the legend below the table, you can determine that a negative difference indicates that Coke had a lower number than Pepsi, and that a positive difference indicates that Coke had a higher number than Pepsi. Since we used lower numbers (1s) to indicate a preference for the brand of pop, you can determine that a negative difference (– sign) indicates a preference for Coke, and a positive difference (+ sign) indicates a preference for Pepsi. Thus, 10 people indicated a preference for Pepsi and only 2 indicated a preference for Coke.

Your Output window will also contain the "Test Statistics" table shown below:

Test Statistics[b]

	Coke - Pepsi
Exact Sig. (2-tailed)	.039[a]

a. Binomial distribution used.

b. Sign Test

The Test Statistics table displays the obtained p value for a two-tailed test in the row labeled "Exact Sig. (2-tailed)." Two-tailed tests are used when the hypothesis is non-directional (meaning you are not predicting the direction of the effect). Since our hypothesis was non-directional (we did not predict which brand would be preferred), this test is appropriate. The p value represents the probability we would obtain these results based on chance alone (if there really isn't a preferred brand of pop). You should be able to clearly see in the above table that our p value is .039. Thus, the probability that this particular result (10 positive differences) or results more extreme would be obtained based on chance alone is .039. Note that all values should generally be rounded to 2 decimal places and the p should be italicized so we would report this p value as, $p = .04$.

Statistically significant effects are those that have a low probability of being a result of chance alone. The alpha level set prior to conducting the experiment represents the probability we are willing to accept making an *incorrect* decision to reject the null hypothesis. A Type I error is when the researcher makes an incorrect decision to reject the null hypothesis. In other words, it is when the researcher concludes the results are statistically significant when really they are just due to chance. So, the alpha level represents the probability the researcher is willing to make a Type I error. Prior to conducting the experiment we decided to set alpha at .05 ($\alpha = .05$), meaning we are willing to accept a 5% chance of making a Type I error (of making an incorrect decision to reject the null hypothesis).

When the obtained p value (the probability the results are due to chance) is equal to or lower than the set alpha level (the probability we are willing to make a Type I error), we can reject the null hypothesis and conclude that the results are statistically significant. If the obtained p value is higher than alpha, we have to retain the null hypothesis and conclude that the results are not statistically significant. Thus, our next step is to compare the p value we obtained ($p = .04$) with the alpha level we set ($\alpha = .05$), to determine whether or not it is appropriate to reject the null hypothesis. Since in this case $p < .05$, we can reject the null hypothesis and conclude that the two brands of pop are not equally preferred (i.e., that one brand is preferred over the other). Moreover, since the number of positive differences outweighs the number of negative differences (and positive differences represent a preference for Pepsi), we can further conclude that Pepsi is preferred over Coke, in taste tests.[3]

Directional Hypotheses and One-Tailed Sign Tests

In the previous example, we used non-directional hypotheses (we didn't predict the direction of effect) and a two-tailed test. For this next example, we will use a directional hypothesis (we will predict the direction of effect) and a one-tailed test.

---

[3] Some interesting research on the Pepsi challenge was conducted because Pepsi typically comes out on top in taste tests, but Coke tends to sell more product than Pepsi. Pepsi is sweeter than Coke, and the results of research indicate that people prefer sweeter drinks (Pepsi) when taking only a sip, but when drinking an entire can they prefer the less sweet Coke. Unfortunately, this discovery was made after Coke spent millions on the sweeter tasting "New Coke" in the 80s—a huge failure for them! For those of you who have taken a research methods course, you may recognize this as an issue of external validity. Taste tests have problems with external validity, because in real life people tend to drink more than a sip.

Imagine you have been hired by a drug company to test the effectiveness of a new sleeping medication called NiteAid. Specifically, the company wants to know whether NiteAid is *more* effective (i.e., puts people to sleep faster) than a placebo. As such, your alternative hypothesis (H_1) is that NiteAid will decrease the number of minutes it takes to fall asleep. Accordingly, your null hypothesis (H_0) is that NiteAid will not decrease the number of minutes it takes to fall asleep. Prior to conducting the study you decide to set alpha at $.05_{1\,tail}$.

Assume you randomly sample 18 individuals from the community and invite each to your sleep lab for 2 nights. You give each individual NiteAid on one night and a placebo on the other night. To guard against order effects, you use complete counterbalancing. You randomly select 9 subjects to take NiteAid on the first night and a placebo on the second night, and 9 subjects to take the placebo on the first night and NiteAid on the second night. Participants are not told which night they are given the placebo or the drug. You measure and record the number of minutes it takes the subject to fall asleep.

Assume you obtain the data shown below:

SUBJECTID	NITEAID	PLACEBO
1	12	21
2	9	16
3	11	8
4	21	36
5	17	28
6	22	20
7	18	29
8	11	22
9	10	21
10	16	19
11	10	15
12	15	9
13	10	22
14	28	32
15	8	12
16	20	18
17	12	12
18	8	8

Begin by entering the data into SPSS. Note that the top row contains the variable names that must be entered in the Variable View window (see Chapter 1). The data in the remaining rows must be entered in Data View (see Chapter 1). Once the data are entered, your Data View window should look like the one displayed on the following page:

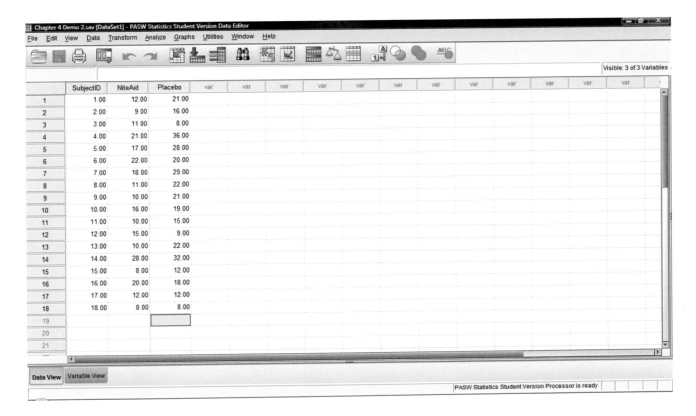

Conducting the Sign Test Analysis

The method for conducting a one-tailed sign test is the same as that for conducting a two-tailed sign test. Using the upper toolbar go to **Analyze → Nonparametric Tests → Legacy Dialogs → 2 Related Samples.** Using the "Two-Related-Samples Tests" dialogue window shown in the adjacent image, highlight the relevant variables— **NiteAid** and **Placebo**—by simply clicking on each variable once. Move the pair over to the **Test Pairs** box by clicking on the **blue arrow. Check** the box labeled **Sign** and **uncheck** the box labeled **Wilcoxon.** Click **OK.**

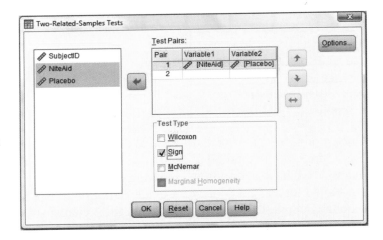

Interpreting the Output

An output window should now appear displaying the following two tables. We'll start by examining the "Frequencies" table shown below:

Frequencies

		N
Placebo - NiteAid	Negative Differences[a]	4
	Positive Differences[b]	12
	Ties[c]	2
	Total	18

a. Placebo < NiteAid

b. Placebo > NiteAid

c. Placebo = NiteAid

From this table you should be able to determine that there are 4 negative differences, 12 positive differences, and 2 ties. The legend shows that a negative difference represents lower scores in the Placebo condition than in the NiteAid condition. Since the data represent the number of minutes it took for subjects to fall asleep, this means that 4 subjects fell asleep faster when they took the placebo. The legend also shows that a positive difference represents lower scores in the NiteAid condition. Therefore, we can determine that 12 subjects fell asleep faster when they took NiteAid. The two ties mean that for 2 subjects there was no difference in the number of minutes it took them to fall asleep. The sign test will not tolerate ties and simply discards the data from ties. Thus, our sample size (n) is now 16 rather than 18.

The "Test Statistics" table is shown below:

Test Statistics[b]

	Placebo - NiteAid
Exact Sig. (2-tailed)	.077[a]

a. Binomial distribution used.

b. Sign Test

Once again, the "Test Statistics" table displays the p value for a two-tailed test in the row labeled "Exact Sig. (2-tailed)." Two-tailed tests are used when the hypothesis is non-directional. However, for this example we have a directional hypothesis, and therefore, we should use a one-tailed test rather than a two-tailed test. SPSS does not provide an option to run a one-tailed sign test, but it is a simple process to manually convert the p value. To obtain the p value for a one-tailed test, simply divide the p value for the two-tailed test in half. For added precision, you should use a p value that has been rounded to at least 4 decimal places. By clicking repeatedly on the value in the table, you should find that the precise p value is .0768. Since $.0768 \div 2 = .0384$, the p value for a one-tailed test is .0384. Once again, this would customarily be rounded to 2 decimal places and reported as, $p = .04$.

Now that we have our obtained p value for a one-tailed test ($p = .04$), our next step is to compare the p value with the alpha level we set ($\alpha = .05_{1\,tail}$) to determine whether or not it is appropriate to reject the null hypothesis. When we use a directional hypothesis, we can only reject the null hypothesis if the results turn out in the predicted direction. We predicted that NiteAid would decrease the number of minutes it takes to fall asleep. As described above, this is represented as a positive difference. Since the number of positive differences outweighed the number of negative differences, we know the results worked out in the predicted direction. Moreover, since $p < .05_{1\,\text{tail}}$, we can reject the null hypothesis and conclude that NiteAid is effective; that it decreases the number of minutes it takes to fall asleep.

You should note that if the results had worked out in the opposite direction to what we predicted, and there were instead 12 negative differences and 4 positive differences (meaning, for most people, NiteAid increased the number of minutes it took to fall asleep), then the displayed p value would be the same. In a case like this we would have to make an adjustment to the p value and retain the null hypothesis. Specifically, we would report the p value as .96 (1 − .0384), and since this value is higher than alpha (.05), we would have to retain the null hypothesis. This demonstrates the risk of using a directional hypothesis, and the importance of examining the direction of effect before reaching a conclusion about whether to reject or retain the null hypothesis.

Single Sample Hypothesis Testing

6

This chapter focuses on single sample hypothesis testing. You will learn how to analyze data using Student's single sample *t*-test. Specifically, you will learn how to conduct the analysis, interpret the output, calculate the confidence interval of the population mean, and report the results in APA style. You will also learn how to report the results of a correlation analysis in APA style, and how to run and interpret the results of a one-tailed correlation test.

Non-Directional Hypotheses and Two-Tailed Single Sample *t*-Tests

According to Statistics Canada's census results, the mean weight of Canadian women was 153lbs in 2005. Imagine you are a researcher interested in examining whether there has been a significant change in the weight of Canadian women since 2005. While obesity rates are currently at an all-time high, you also recognize that many Canadians are beginning to adopt healthier lifestyles. As such, you decide to use a non-directional hypothesis. Your alternative hypothesis (H_1) is that there has been a significant change in the mean weight of Canadian women since 2005. Accordingly, your null hypothesis (H_0) is that there has not been a significant change in the mean weight of Canadian women since 2005. Prior to collecting any data you decide to stick with the convention and set alpha at .05.

Assume you randomly sampled 30 women from the general population of Canada and obtained the following data on their weights (in lbs):

SUBJECTID	WEIGHT	SUBJECTID	WEIGHT	SUBJECTID	WEIGHT
1	165	11	149	21	129
2	110	12	136	22	117
3	107	13	212	23	152
4	163	14	157	24	183
5	195	15	132	25	169
6	159	16	128	26	145
7	168	17	178	27	265
8	145	18	210	28	162
9	125	19	159	29	179
10	198	20	195	30	285

Begin by opening SPSS and entering in the 30 women's subject IDs and weights into two columns in the Data View window. Note that the top row contains the variable names that must be entered in the Variable View window (see Chapter 1). While you are in Variable View, you should define the properties of the variables. Once the data are entered, your Data View window should look like the one shown on the following page.

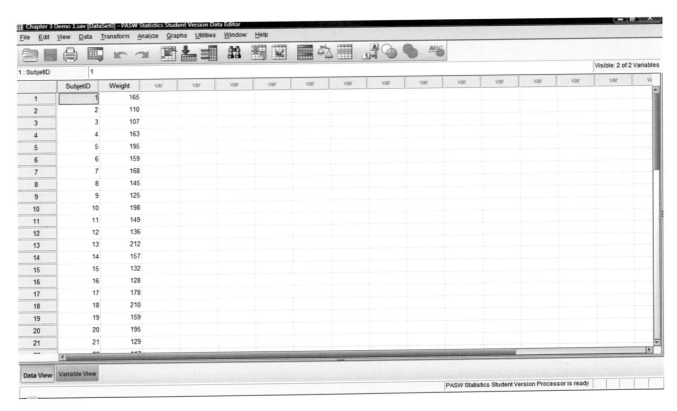

Conducting the Single Sample *t*-Test Analysis

To conduct the single sample *t*-test, simply use the upper toolbar to go to **Analyze → Compare Means → One-Sample T Test.**

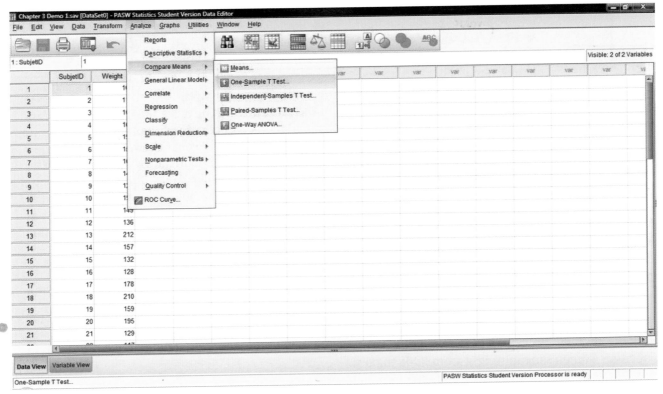

A "One-Sample T Test" dialogue window, like the one shown on the right, will now appear. Using the dialogue window, highlight the relevant variable—**Weight**—by clicking on the variable name, and move it over to the **Test Variable(s) box** by clicking the **blue arrow**. Next, enter the population mean—**153**—into the **Test Value box**. Click **OK** to close the dialogue box and execute the analysis.

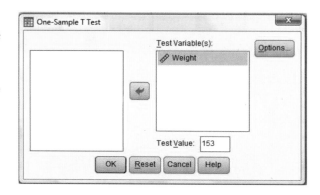

Interpreting the Output

An Output window should now appear displaying two tables. Let's first examine the "One-Sample Statistics" table shown below:

One-Sample Statistics

	N	Mean	Std. Deviation	Std. Error Mean
Weight	30	165.90	40.884	7.464

The first column simply displays the name of the variable you are considering in the analysis. The column labeled "N" displays the number of subjects in the sample. The column labeled "Mean" displays the sample's mean weight, and the column labeled "Std. Deviation" displays the standard deviation of the sample weights. Finally, the column labeled "Std. Error Mean" displays the standard deviation of the sampling distribution of the mean, which is also known as the standard error of the mean.

Let's now consider the "One-Sample Test" table shown below:

One-Sample Test

	Test Value = 153					
			p-value Sig. (2-tailed)	Mean Difference	95% Confidence Interval of the Difference	
	T	df			Lower	Upper
Weight	1.728	29	.095	12.900	-2.37	28.17

The primary results of the analysis are presented in this table. The mean of the population to which we are comparing our sample is provided at the very top of the table next to the label "Test Value." You can use this to confirm that you entered in the mean of the population correctly. Next, looking at the columns you should see a column labeled "T," which provides the obtained t value. From this we can determine that t = 1.728. The next column labeled "df" gives us our degrees of freedom; it shows that we have 29 degrees of freedom. The column labeled "Sig. (2-tailed)" shows the precise p value. The table shows that the p value is .095, meaning that the probability that these results would be obtained by chance alone is .095 (9.5%). The column labeled "Mean Difference" displays the difference between the sample mean and the population mean. The value indicates that our sample has a mean weight that is 12.90lbs higher than the population's mean weight.

The last two columns of the "One-Sample Test" table provide the lower and upper limits of the 95% confidence interval for the *mean difference*. The 95% confidence interval for the mean difference provides a range of values for which you can be 95% certain contains the true difference between the sample and population means. Thus, the 95% confidence interval for the mean difference displayed in the table indicates that we can be 95% certain that the interval –2.37lbs to 28.17lbs contains the true difference in Canadian women's mean weight from 2005 to now.

Calculating Confidence Intervals for the Population Mean

Researchers are often interested in obtaining the confidence interval for the *population mean* (rather than the confidence interval for the mean difference). The 95% confidence interval for the population mean, provides a range of values for which you can be 95% certain contains the true population mean. This is a subtle but important distinction from the 95% confidence interval for the mean difference. SPSS only provides the confidence interval for the mean difference. The confidence interval for the population mean can easily be hand-calculated using some of the values in the table. Specifically, to calculate the 95% confidence interval for the population mean, we will need the sample mean ($\overline{X}_{obt}$), the standard error of the mean ($s_{\overline{X}}$), and the critical t value for an alpha of .05 ($t_{.025}$). As described above, the sample mean and the standard error of the mean can both be found in the "One-Sample Statistics" table. To determine the critical t value, you will need to refer to a table of the Critical Values of Student's t Distribution. For a two-tailed test and alpha of .05, the critical t value is 2.045. The formulas for calculating the lower and upper limits of the confidence interval for the population mean are provided below. Let's go ahead and practice hand-calculating the confidence interval for the population mean.

$$\mu_{lower} = \overline{X}_{obt} - s_{\overline{X}} \ (t_{.025}) = 165.90 - 7.4645(2.045) = 165.90 - 15.2649 = 150.64$$

$$\mu_{upper} = \overline{X}_{obt} + s_{\overline{X}} \ (t_{.025}) = 165.90 + 7.4645(2.045) = 165.90 + 15.2649 = 181.16$$

Reporting the Results

According to APA style (the style of the American Psychological Association), the results of t-tests are reported using the following format $t(df) = ?.??, p = .??$. There are two question marks serving as placeholders after the decimal points, because APA style requires us to round decimal remainders to 2 places (unless the value is less than .01). APA style also requires us to italicize all statistical notation, so the t is an italicized t and the p is an italicized p. The number of degrees of freedom is reported in brackets next to the italicized t. The obtained t value is reported next. A comma is placed after the obtained t value, and then the exact p value is reported. For the analysis we conducted we would report the following: $t(29) = 1.73, p = .09$. Since $p > .05$, we must retain the null hypothesis and conclude that there has been no significant change in the mean weight of Canadian women since 2005.

Confidence intervals are typically reported using the following style: ??% CI = ??.?? to ??.??. Based on the results of our hand calculation of the 95% confidence interval we would report the following: 95% CI = 150.64 to 181.16. Our conclusion based on this confidence interval is that we can be 95% certain that the true mean weight of the current population of Canadian women is between 150.64lbs and 181.16lbs. Since the mean weight of the population of Canadian women in 2005 (153lbs) is contained within this interval, we must retain the null hypothesis, and conclude that there has not been a significant change in the mean weight of Canadian women since 2005. You can see that using either the traditional (p value) method or the alternative confidence interval method, we will arrive at the same decision to reject or retain the null hypothesis, and therefore, the same conclusion.

Directional Hypotheses and One-Tailed Single Sample t-Tests

Let's now assume that you are a dietician who has growing concerns about the impact of the rapid growth of the fast food industry on Canadian women's weight. As such, you are only interested in whether the mean weight of Canadian women has *increased* since 2005. Your alternative hypothesis is that the mean weight of Canadian women has increased since 2005. Accordingly, your null hypothesis is that the mean weight of Canadian women has not increased since 2005. Assume that prior to collecting any data you decide to set alpha at .05$_{1\,tail}$. You randomly sample the same 30 Canadian women whose data appear at the beginning of this chapter.[1]

Conducting the Single Sample *t*-Test Analysis

SPSS does not provide an option to conduct a one-tailed Single Sample *t*-test, so directional hypotheses do not influence the way we conduct the analysis. We still go to **Analyze → Compare Means → One-Sample T Test**. We still highlight the relevant variable—**Weight**—by clicking on the variable name, and we move it over to the **Test Variable(s)** box by clicking the **blue arrow**. We enter the same population mean—**153**—into the **Test Value box** by typing in the number and then click **OK** to initiate the analysis.

Interpreting the Output

Since the analysis is identical to the one we previously conducted, the same two tables will now appear in the Output window. They are once again shown below:

One-Sample Statistics

	N	Mean	Std. Deviation	Std. Error Mean
Weight	30	165.90	40.884	7.464

One-Sample Test

	Test Value = 153					
					95% Confidence Interval of the Difference	
	T	df	Sig. (2-tailed)	Mean Difference	Lower	Upper
Weight	1.728	29	.095	12.900	-2.37	28.17

What differs with directional hypotheses is the manner in which we interpret the *p* value displayed in the "One-Sample Test" table. The *p* value provided in the table is for a two-tailed test (non-directional hypothesis). To adjust it for our one-tailed test (directional hypothesis), all we need to do is divide it in half. Let's go ahead and do that: .0946 ÷ 2 = .0473. Thus, our *p* value for a one-tailed test is .0473. Before we reach any conclusions, we need to examine whether our results are in the predicted direction. Our obtained sample mean (shown in the "One-Sample Statistics" table) is 165.90, and our population mean (shown at the very top of the "One-Sample Test" table) is 153. Since our sample mean is higher than our population mean, we know that the results are in the predicted direction.

---

[1] Note that this directional hypothesis would have had to been made before collecting any data. It is scientific cheating to switch from a non-directional to a directional hypothesis after seeing the results! In the long run, practicing this type of cheating will inflate your Type I error rate to 7.5%.

Reporting the Results

Using APA style we can now report the following results: $t(29) = 1.73$, $p = .047$.[2] Since $p < .05$, we can reject the null hypothesis and conclude that there has been a significant increase in the mean weight of Canadian women since 2005.

Predicting the Wrong Direction

It is important to note what would change if we had made a prediction in the wrong direction. Let's assume we had predicted a *decrease* in the mean weight of Canadian women, but that we obtained the same results we've been considering here (showing an *increase* in the mean weight of Canadian women). In this case, our calculation of the p value would change. Rather than simply dividing the p value by 2, as we did when the results worked out in the predicted direction, we would now need to subtract the divided p value from a value of 1. So, we would still divide the p value by 2 ($.0946 \div 2 = .0473$), but now we would need to subtract the result from a value of 1 ($1 - .0473 = .9527$), because our outcome is in the opposite tail as we predicted. In this case we would report the following: $t(29) = 1.73$, $p = .95$. Since $p > .05$ in this scenario, we would need to retain the null hypothesis and conclude that there has not been a significant decrease in the mean weight of Canadian women since 2005.

Non-Directional Hypotheses and Two-Tailed Correlation Analyses

Now that you are starting to get a feel for hypothesis testing, we will return briefly to the topic of correlation and review how to determine whether a correlation coefficient is significant, how to report the results of a correlation analysis in APA style, and how to run a one-tailed correlation analysis.

We will once again use the "Employee data.sav" sample data file that we used in Chapters 3 and 4. Begin by opening the data file (see the section of Chapter 3 on Opening A Sample Data File to review how to open this file if necessary).

Let's assume we are interested in whether there is a significant correlation between people's current salaries and the number of months they've been employed in the job. Our alternative hypothesis is that there is a correlation between current salary and number of months of employment. Accordingly, our null hypothesis is that there is not a correlation between current salary and number of months of employment. Once again, we will stick with convention and set alpha at .05.

Conducting a Two-Tailed Correlation Analysis

If you will recall from Chapter 3, in order to conduct the correlation analysis you simply need to go to **Analyze → Correlate → Bivariate**. A dialogue window labeled "Bivariate Correlations" will then appear. Using the dialogue window, click on the variable **Current Salary** and press the **blue arrow** to move it

---

[2] Since the p value of .047 rounds to .05, we will report the value rounded to 3 decimal places. This way, our readers/reviewers will know that our value is under .05 (and not simply between .051 and .054, which would not be considered significant).

into the **Variables box**, then click on the variable **Months since Hire** and press the **blue arrow** to move it into the **Variables box**. Finally, press **OK** to initiate the analysis.

Interpreting the Output

The following "Correlations" table will now appear in the Output window:

Correlations

		Current Salary	Months since Hire
Current Salary	Pearson Correlation	1.000	.084
	Sig. (2-tailed)		.067
	N	474	474
Months since Hire	Pearson Correlation	.084	1.000
	Sig. (2-tailed)	.067	
	N	474	474

As you learned in Chapter 3, the rows labeled "Pearson Correlation" display the correlation coefficients, the rows labeled "Sig. (2-tailed)" contain the p values, and the rows labeled "N" show the sample size (i.e., the number of people included in the analysis). You should be able to see that the correlation between Current Salary and Months since Hire is .084, that the p value is .067, and that the sample size is 474.

Reporting the Results

The results of correlation analyses are reported using the following format $r(df) = .??, p = .??$. Remember that APA style requires us to round our decimal remainders to 2 decimal places (unless the value is less than .01) and to italicize all statistical notation. So, the r shown is an italicized r. The degrees of freedom are not provided in the output table, but degrees of freedom for correlations are equal to the size of the sample minus 2 ($df = n - 2$). As described above, the sample size is 474, so our degrees of freedom are 474 − 2 = 472. The r obtained value is reported next *without* a 0 before the decimal point. A comma is placed after the obtained r value, followed by the exact p value. So, for the results obtained above, we would report the following: $r(472) = .08, p = .07$. Since $p > .05$, we must retain the null hypothesis and conclude that there is not a correlation between current salary and number of months since hire.

Directional Hypotheses and One-Tailed Correlation Analyses

Let's now assume we are only interested in whether there is a significant *positive* correlation between people's current salaries and the number of months since they've been hired. Our alternative hypothesis is that there is a positive correlation between current salary and number of months since hire. Accordingly, our null hypothesis is that there is not a positive correlation between current salary and months since hire. Once again, we will stick with convention and set alpha at $.05_{1\,tail}$.

Conducting a One-Tailed Correlation Analysis

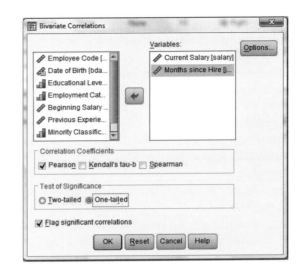

SPSS does provide an option to execute a one-tailed correlation analysis, so directional hypotheses do slightly change the way we analyze the data in SPSS. We still go to **Analyze → Correlate → Bivariate**. We still use the "Bivariate Correlations" dialogue box and put **Current Salary** and **Months since Hire** in the **Variables box** using the **blue arrow**. But, to run a one-tailed test we now need to click on **One-tailed** under the heading "Test of Significance" before clicking **OK**.

Interpreting the Output

The following table will now appear in the Output window:

Correlations

		Current Salary	Months since Hire
Current Salary	Pearson Correlation	1.000	.084*
	Sig. (1-tailed)		.034
	N	474.000	474
Months since Hire	Pearson Correlation	.084*	1.000
	Sig. (1-tailed)	.034	
	N	474	474.000

*. Correlation is significant at the 0.05 level (1-tailed).

As you can see, the correlation coefficient does not change; it is still .084. What changes is the p value. The p value provided is now for a one-tailed test, so we do not need to manually adjust it as we did for the Sign Test and the Single Sample t-Test. Thus, you can directly see in the table that our p value for this one-tailed test is .034. Before making any conclusions, we need to check to make sure that the correlation is in the same direction as we predicted: and indeed, it is in the positive direction.

Reporting the Results

Using APA style, we can now report the following results: $r(472) = .08$, $p = .03$. Since $p < .05$, we can now reject the null hypothesis and conclude that there is a small positive correlation between current salary and number of months since hire.

Predicting the Wrong Direction

It is important to note that SPSS does not know which direction we are predicting, even when we use the option to run a one-tailed test. SPSS always assumes that our prediction is in the correct direction (the direction the results end up falling), so it is important to consider how things would change if we predicted the wrong direction. Assume our alternative hypothesis was that there is a *negative* correlation between current salary and number of months since hire. Our null hypothesis would then be that there is not a negative correlation between current salary and number of months since hire.

If we were to run the one-tailed correlation analysis, we would get the same "Correlations" table shown on the preceding page, indicating a positive correlation of .08 and a p value of .03. However, since the results turned out in the opposite direction to what we predicted (in this scenario we are predicting a negative correlation, but the results show a positive correlation), we would need to adjust the p value by subtracting it from 1. So, the p value that we would report would be $1 - .0337 = .9663$. Thus, our reported results in this scenario would be $r(472) = .08$, $p = .97$. Since $p > 05$, we would need to retain the null hypothesis and conclude that there is not a negative correlation between current salary and months since hire. Note: we *cannot* conclude that there is a significant positive correlation between the variables. This is the risk we take when we make a directional hypothesis. If the results turn out to be significant in the opposite direction, we must adjust the p value and retain the null hypothesis.

Student's *t*-Tests for Correlated and Independent Groups

7

In this chapter you will learn how to analyze data using Student's *t*-tests for correlated and independent groups. Specifically, you will learn how to conduct the analyses, interpret the output, and report the results in APA style.

Student's *t*-Test for Correlated Groups

Assume you are a researcher interested in the acute effects of marijuana (i.e., the effects of being high on marijuana) on memory test performance. Your alternative hypothesis (H_1) is that marijuana will affect memory test performance. Accordingly, your null hypothesis (H_0) is that marijuana will not affect memory test performance. Prior to conducting the study you decide to set alpha at .05.

Assume that you decide to use a repeated measures design.[1] You randomly select and invite 20 individuals to your lab on two separate days. Each individual is given a joint containing THC (i.e., the active ingredient in marijuana) to smoke on one day, and a placebo joint that doesn't contain any THC to smoke on the other day. Participants are not informed which day they smoke the joint that contains the THC. To guard against order effects, you use complete counterbalancing. Half of the participants smoke the joint containing THC on Day 1 and the placebo joint on Day 2, and the other half of the participants smoke the placebo joint on Day 1 and the joint containing THC on Day 2. Immediately, after smoking each of the joints, participants are given a memory test. They are read a list of 15 words and are asked to recall as many words from the list as possible. You measure and record the number of words each subject correctly recalls.

Assume you obtain the data shown below:

SUBJECTID	THC	PLACEBO	SUBJECTID	THC	PLACEBO
1	7	8	11	6	8
2	5	7	12	5	7
3	4	5	13	9	12
4	12	10	14	12	12
5	8	9	15	15	12
6	9	11	16	7	9
7	11	13	17	5	7
8	6	5	18	9	11
9	7	9	19	10	8
10	8	8	20	5	6

Begin by entering the data into SPSS. Note that the top row contains the variable names that must be entered in the Variable View window (see Chapter 1). The data in the remaining rows must be entered in 3 columns in the Data View window (see Chapter 1). Once the data are entered, your Data View window should look like the one displayed on the following page.

---

[1] The correlated groups *t*-test requires the use of a repeated measures (i.e., within-subject) design.

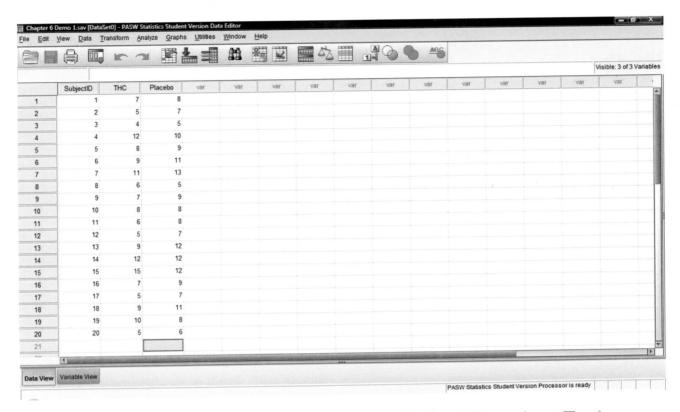

Conducting a *t*-Test for Correlated Groups (Paired Samples *t*-Test)

To conduct a *t*-test for correlated groups you need to go to **Analyze → Compare Means → Paired-Samples T Test**.

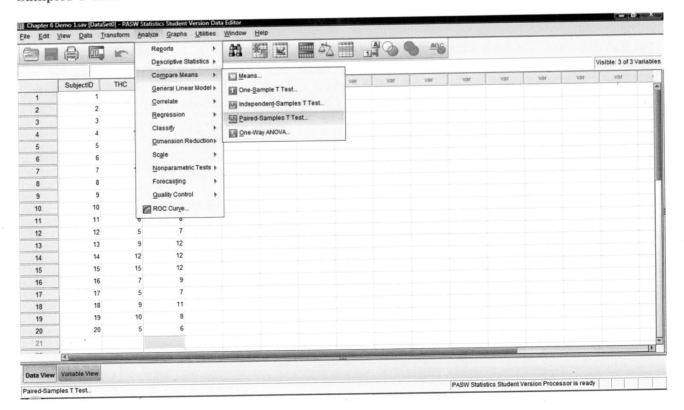

A "Paired-Samples T Test" dialogue window, like the one shown below, will now appear. Highlight the relevant variables—**THC** and **Placebo**—by clicking on each of the variable names and then click on the **blue arrow** to move them over to the **Paired Variables box**. Click **OK** to initiate the analysis.

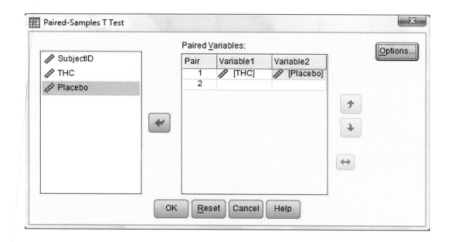

Interpreting the Output

A series of tables will then appear in the Output window. We will first examine the "Paired-Samples Statistics" table shown below:

Paired Samples Statistics

		Mean	N	Std. Deviation	Std. Error Mean
Pair 1	THC	8.00	20	2.902	.649
	Placebo	8.85	20	2.390	.534

This table provides some basic descriptive statistics. The first column in the table displays the variables that are being compared. The column labeled "Mean" shows the means for each condition. From this column you should be able to determine that participants were able to recall a mean of 8.00 words in the THC condition and a mean of 8.85 words in the Placebo condition. The column labeled "N" displays the number of participants in each condition. Since we are considering data from a repeated measures design, there should always be an equal number of participants in each of the conditions. The column labeled "Std. Deviation" presents the standard deviation for each condition. Finally, the column labeled "Std. Error Mean" provides the standard error of the mean for each group/condition.

The next table we will examine is the "Paired Samples Correlations" table shown below:

Paired Samples Correlations

		N	Correlation	Sig.
Pair 1	THC & Placebo	20	.819	.000

This table displays the correlation between the scores in the two conditions. You can see by looking at this table that there is a large positive correlation, $r(18) = .82$, $p < .001^2$, between the number of words subjects were able to recall after smoking a joint containing THC and the number of words they were able to recall after smoking a placebo joint.

Finally, your Output window should display the "Paired Samples Test" table shown below:

Paired Samples Test

				95% Confidence Interval of the Difference				
		Std.	Std. Error					Sig.
	Mean	Deviation	Mean	Lower	Upper	t	df	(2-tailed)
Pair 1 THC - Placebo	-.850	1.663	.372	-1.628	-.072	-2.286	19	.034

This table provides us with all of the information we need to report and interpret the results. Once again, the first column displays the conditions being compared as well as which scores were subtracted from which. You should be able to see that scores in the Placebo condition were subtracted from scores in the THC condition. The column labeled "Mean" shows the mean of the difference scores. Since scores in the Placebo condition were subtracted from scores in the THC condition, the negative difference score (–.85) indicates that scores in the THC condition were lower than scores in the Placebo condition. More precisely, the value indicates that on average participants were able to recall .85 fewer words after smoking the joint containing THC. The column labeled "Std. Deviation" provides the standard deviation of the difference scores, and the column labeled "Std. Error Mean" displays the estimated standard deviation of the sampling distribution of the difference between sample means. The section of the table labeled "95% Confidence Interval of the Difference" presents the lower and upper limits of the 95% confidence interval for the difference in means. The column labeled "t" displays the obtained *t* value. The column labeled "df" gives the degrees of freedom, and the column labeled "Sig. (2-tailed)" provides the *p* value for a two-tailed test.

Reporting the Results

All of the information we need to report the findings using APA style can be found in the last three columns of the "Paired Samples Test" table. As described above, these columns display the obtained *t* value (–2.286), the degrees of freedom (19), and the precise *p* value for a two-tailed test (.034). Using APA style, we should report the following: $t(19) = -2.29$, $p = .03$. Since $p < .05$, we can reject the null hypothesis and conclude that marijuana has an acute effect on memory test performance.

As described above, the "Paired Samples Test" table also provides the lower and upper limits of the 95% confidence interval for the difference in means. We would report the confidence interval in the following manner: 95% CI = –1.63 to –.07. Thus, we can be 95% certain that the interval –1.63 to –.07 contains the true acute effect of marijuana on memory test performance. In other words we can be 95% certain that being high on marijuana decreases memory test performance by .07 to 1.63 recalled words. Since the confidence interval does not cross 0, we can reject the null hypothesis and conclude that marijuana has an acute effect on memory test performance.

---

[2] While it is preferable to report the exact *p* value, because this *p* value is so low (.0000098), the traditional method of reporting the *p* value relative to alpha is shown here.

Confidence Intervals for the Difference in Means

By default, SPSS provides the 95% confidence interval because it is the most commonly used confidence interval. However, you can change this setting and request any confidence interval you'd like. Let's practice by changing the setting so we can obtain the 99% confidence interval. To change the confidence interval, go to **Analyze → Compare Means → Paired-Samples T Test.** Highlight the relevant variables—**THC** and **Placebo**—by clicking on the variable names, and click the **blue arrow** to move them over to the **Paired Variables box.** Next, click the **Options box.** A "Paired-Samples T Test: Options" window like the one shown on the right will now appear. Replace the value of 95 with a value of **99** by simply typing in the white box. Press **Continue** to close that dialogue window and press **OK** to run the analysis.

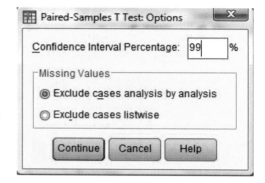

The same three tables will appear in the output window. The only difference between these tables and the ones we produced previously will be in the "Paired Samples Test" table shown below:

Paired Samples Test

					99% Confidence Interval of the Difference				
		Mean	Std. Deviation	Std. Error Mean	Lower	Upper	T	df	Sig. (2-tailed)
Pair 1	THC – Placebo	-.850	1.663	.372	-1.914	.214	-2.286	19	.034

You should note that nothing in the table has changed except for the confidence interval. The table now displays the 99% confidence interval for the difference in means (rather than the default 95% confidence interval). The 99% confidence interval would be reported in the following manner: 99% CI = −1.91 to .21. According to this confidence interval, we can be 99% certain that the interval −1.91 to .21 contains the true acute effect of marijuana on memory test performance. Since this confidence interval does cross 0, we must retain the null hypothesis and conclude that being high on marijuana does not have an effect on memory test performance. Note that we would have reached this same conclusion using the traditional p value method and an alpha of .01 (the alpha level that corresponds to the 99% confidence interval), because $p = .03 > .01$.

Student's *t*-Test for Independent Groups

A previous president of Harvard University once publically speculated that one reason why women are underrepresented in the sciences is because of a "different availability of aptitude at the high end." In other words, he claimed that women are underrepresented in the sciences because they do not have the innate abilities necessary to excel in them. Let's assume you are a researcher who is infuriated by this statement because you think statements like these adversely affect women. As such, you decide to examine the influence of claims like this one on women's actual math test performance.

Assume that in order to examine the influence of statements like the one made by Harvard's former president you decide to use an independent groups design.[3] You invite 20 women to your lab and you randomly assign each woman to one of two separate conditions. Women in both conditions are told to wait in a waiting area where they "accidently overhear" a staged conversation between two professors. Women in Condition 1 (the genetic condition), "accidently overhear" the professors discussing a new paper revealing evidence that a math gene has been discovered, which is sex-linked and commonly deficient in women. Women in Condition 2 (the socialization condition), "accidently overhear" the professors discussing a new paper, revealing evidence that women only tend to perform worse on math tests because they are raised in a society where women are regarded as being inferior at math. After participants overhear one of these discussions, they are asked to complete a math test containing 20 questions. Your alternative hypothesis (H_1) is that women's math test performance will be affected by the message they overhear. Accordingly, your null hypothesis (H_0) is that women's math test performance will not be affected by the message they overhear. Prior to collecting any data you decide to set alpha at .05.

Assume you record the following math test scores:

SUBJECTID	CONDITION	MATH SCORE	SUBJECTID	CONDITION	MATH SCORE
1	1	15	11	1	8
2	2	18	12	2	20
3	1	12	13	1	12
4	2	13	14	2	16
5	1	11	15	1	14
6	2	10	16	2	11
7	1	15	17	1	9
8	2	17	18	2	16
9	1	14	19	1	16
10	2	19	20	2	20

Begin by entering the data into SPSS. Note that the top row contains the variable names that must be entered in the Variable View window (see Chapter 1). The data in the remaining rows must be entered in 3 columns in the Data View window (see Chapter 1). Once the data are entered, your Data View window should look like the one displayed on the following page:

---

[3] The independent groups *t*-test requires the use of an independent groups (i.e., between-subjects) design.

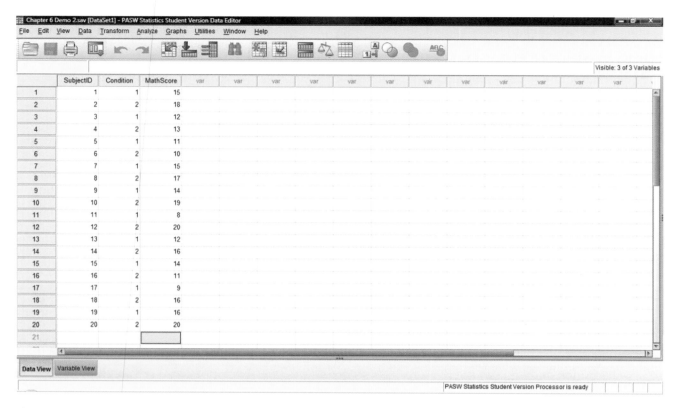

Conducting the *t*-Test for Independent Groups

To conduct a *t*-test for independent groups, you need to use the upper toolbar to go to **Analyze →
Compare Means → Independent-Samples T Test.**

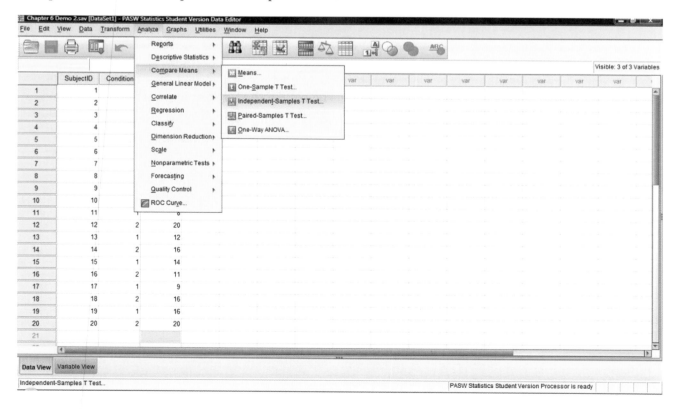

Next, an "Independent-Samples T Test" dialogue window, like the one shown below, will open. Highlight the dependent variable—**MathScore**—by clicking on the variable name, and click the corresponding **blue arrow** to move it over to the **Test Variable(s) box**. Next, highlight the independent variable— **Condition**—by clicking on the variable name, and move it over to the **Grouping Variable box** by clicking the corresponding **blue arrow**. Next, click on the **Define Groups tab**.

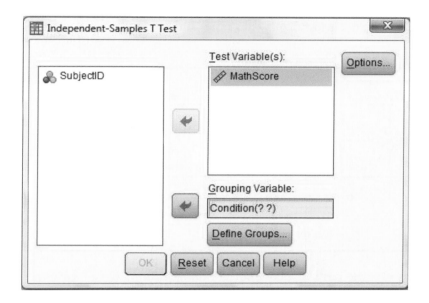

A "Define Groups" dialogue window like the one shown on the right will now appear. You will need to use this box to specify the values used to designate the different levels of the independent variable. Since we used 1s and 2s to identify participants in the two conditions, you should enter **1** into the box labeled **Group 1** and **2** into the box labeled **Group 2**. Close the dialogue window by clicking **Continue**. Next, click **OK** to close the "Independent-Samples T Test" dialogue window and initiate the analysis.

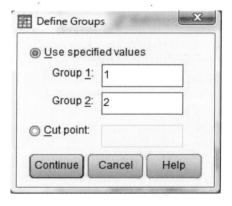

Interpreting the Output

An Output window should now appear displaying the following tables. We will first examine the "Group Statistics" table shown below:

Group Statistics

	Condition	N	Mean	Std. Deviation	Std. Error Mean
MathScore	1	10	12.60	2.675	.846
	2	10	16.00	3.590	1.135

This first column of the table presents the dependent variable under consideration—MathScore—as well as information on which condition mean was subtracted from which, to obtain the mean difference score. You should be able to see from the information provided in this column that the mean math test score in Condition 2 was subtracted from the mean math test score in Condition 1. The table values in the second row correspond to Condition 1 and the table values in the third row correspond to Condition 2. The column labeled "N" shows the number of subjects in each condition (there were 10 subjects in each condition). The column labeled "Mean" displays the mean math test score in each of the two conditions. You should be able to see that the mean math test score of women in Condition 1 (the genetics condition) was 12.60, and the mean math test score of women in Condition 2 (the socialization condition) was 16.00. The column labeled "Std. Deviation" shows the standard deviation of scores in each condition. Finally, the column labeled "Std. Error Mean" provides the standard error of the mean for each condition.

The primary results of the analysis are displayed in the "Independent Samples Test" table shown below:

Independent Samples Test

| | | Levene's Test for Equality of Variances | | t-test for Equality of Means | | | | | | |
		F	Sig.	t	df	Sig. (2-tailed)	Mean Difference	Std. Error Difference	95% Confidence Interval of the Difference Lower	Upper
Math	Equal variances assumed	.604	.447	-2.401	18	.027	-3.400	1.416	-6.374	-.426
	Equal variances not assumed			-2.401	16.639	.028	-3.400	1.416	-6.392	-.408

The first several columns of the table display information pertaining to the variances of the samples (the variance is simply the standard deviation squared). An assumption underlying the t-test for independent groups is homogeneity of variance. If the variances of the two groups/conditions are highly dissimilar, then this assumption has been violated. If the variances of the two groups/conditions are similar, then this assumption has been met. By default, SPSS tests this assumption whenever you conduct a t-test for independent groups. The test SPSS uses to assess whether this assumption has been violated is called Levene's test for equality of variances. If the results of Levene's test are significant ($p < .05$), then the variances are significantly different, meaning the data violate the assumption of homogeneity of variance. SPSS suggests you report the adjusted values in the last row (the row labeled "Equal variances not assumed") when the assumption has been violated. If the results of Levene's test are not significant ($p > .05$), then the variances are not significantly different, meaning the assumption has been met. We do not worry too much about violating this assumption, because the independent groups t-test is robust to (i.e., affected very little by) violations of this assumption, especially when the same number of subjects are used in each group/condition (i.e., when $n_1 = n_2$). Provided you have equal sized groups, you can simply report the results in the first row regardless of the outcome of Levene's test. You can see by looking at the column labeled "Sig.," that for our analysis the result of Levene's test was not significant ($p > .05$). Hence, we can conclude that our two groups have similar variances, and as such, that the assumption of homogeneity of variance has been met.

The column labeled "t" displays the obtained t value. The column labeled "df" gives the degrees of freedom, and the column labeled "Sig. (2-tailed)" provides the p value for a two-tailed test. The next piece of information we can extract from the table is the difference in the means of the two groups, which is presented in the column labeled "Mean Difference." Before we can interpret what this value means, we need to consider which mean was subtracted from which, to obtain the mean difference score. If you'll recall, the "Group Statistics" table provided us with this information; it showed that the mean of Condition 2 was subtracted from the mean of Condition 1. Thus, the negative mean difference value reported in the table shown above indicates that the mean of the math test scores of women in Condition 1 (genetics condition) was 3.40 points below the mean of the math test scores of women in Condition 2 (socialization condition). The column labeled "Std. Error Difference" provides the standard error of the mean for the difference scores (which is the estimated standard deviation of the sampling distribution of the difference between sample means). Finally, the last section of the table, labeled "95% Confidence Interval of the Difference," gives you the lower and upper limits of the 95% confidence interval for the difference in means.

Reporting the Results

All of the information we need to report the findings using APA style can be found in the middle three columns of the "Independent Samples Test" table. These columns display the obtained *t* value (–2.401), the degrees of freedom (18), and the precise *p* value for a two-tailed test (.027). Using APA style, we should report the following: $t(18) = -2.40$, $p = .03$. Since $p < .05$, we can reject the null hypothesis and conclude that women's math test performance was affected by the message they overheard. Since the mean math test score was lower in Condition 1 (genetics condition), we can further conclude that statements that they have a genetic disadvantage adversely affect women's math test performance.[4]

As described earlier, the "Independent Samples Test" table also provides the lower and upper limits of the 95% confidence interval for the difference in means. We would report the confidence interval in the following manner: 95% CI = –6.37 to –.43. Thus, we can be 95% certain that the interval –6.37 to –.43 contains the true effect of the statement that women are genetically predisposed to be poor at math on women's actual math test performance. In other words, we can be 95% certain that exposure to genetic explanations for women's math abilities decreases their math performance by .43 to 6.37 points. Since the confidence interval does not cross 0, we can reject the null hypothesis and conclude that statements that they have a genetic disadvantage adversely affect women's math test performance.

Confidence Intervals for the Difference in Means

Once again, by default SPSS provides the 95% confidence interval for the difference in means. However, this setting can easily be changed to produce any confidence interval you'd like. Let's practice changing this setting by requesting the 99% confidence interval. Go to **Analyze → Compare Means → Independent-Samples T Test**. Using the "Independent-Samples T Test" dialogue window, highlight the variable **Math** by clicking on the variable name, and then click the **blue arrow** to move it over to the **Test Variables box**. Next, highlight the variable **Condition** by clicking on it, and then click on the **blue arrow** to move it over to the **Grouping Variable box**. Next, click on the **Define Groups box**, and using the "Define Groups" dialogue window, specify your values. Once again, since we used 1s and 2s to identify the conditions, enter **1** into box labeled **Group 1** and **2** into the box labeled **Group 2**. Close the "Define Groups" dialogue window by clicking **Continue**. Next, click the **Options box** in the "Independent-Samples T Test" dialogue window. An "Independent-Samples T Test: Options" dialogue window like the one shown on the right will now open. Replace the value of 95 with a value of **99** by simply typing in the box. Press **Continue** to close the dialogue window and press **OK** to run the analysis.

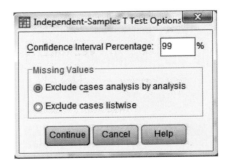

[4] While the data presented in this guide were all fabricated, this example was inspired by a real study conducted by researchers at the University of British Columbia. The researchers of this study found results similar to the ones presented here. The reference for the paper is: Dar-Nimrod, I., & Heine, S. J. (2006). Exposure to scientific theories affects women's math performance. *Science*, 314, 435. DOI: 10.1126/science.1131100

The same tables will appear in the Output window. The only difference between these tables and the ones we produced previously are in the "Independent Samples Test" table shown below:

Independent Samples Test

		Levene's Test for Equality of Variances		t-test for Equality of Means						99% Confidence Interval of the Difference	
		F	Sig.	t	df	Sig. (2-tailed)	Mean Difference	Std. Error Difference		Lower	Upper
Math	Equal variances assumed	.604	.447	-2.401	18	.027	-3.400	1.416		-7.475	.675
	Equal variances not assumed			-2.401	16.639	.028	-3.400	1.416		-7.514	.714

You should note that nothing in the table has changed except for the confidence interval. The table now displays the 99% confidence interval for the difference in means. The 99% confidence interval would be reported in the following manner: 99% CI = −7.48 to .68. According to this confidence interval we can be 99% certain that the interval −7.48 to .68 contains the true effect of the statement that women are genetically predisposed to be poor at math on women's actual math test performance. Since the confidence interval does cross 0, we must retain the null hypothesis and conclude that the effect is not statistically significant. Note that we would have reached this same conclusion using the traditional p value method and an alpha of .01 (the alpha level, which corresponds to the 99% confidence interval), because $p = .03 > .01$.

Congratulations! You have now mastered some of the most commonly used functions in SPSS! There are many other analyses and functions that SPSS is capable of performing that you may wish to begin to explore on your own or with the assistance of the tutorial function which can be found under the Help menu in the upper toolbar.